Kant and Theodicy

Kant and Theodicy

A Search for an Answer to the Problem of Evil

George Huxford

LEXINGTON BOOKS
Lanham • Boulder • New York • London

Published by Lexington Books
An imprint of The Rowman & Littlefield Publishing Group, Inc.
4501 Forbes Boulevard, Suite 200, Lanham, Maryland 20706
www.rowman.com

6 Tinworth Street, London SE11 5AL, United Kingdom

Copyright © 2020 The Rowman & Littlefield Publishing Group, Inc.

All rights reserved. No part of this book may be reproduced in any form or by any electronic or mechanical means, including information storage and retrieval systems, without written permission from the publisher, except by a reviewer who may quote passages in a review.

British Library Cataloguing in Publication Information Available

Library of Congress Cataloging-in-Publication Data Available

ISBN: 978-1-4985-9723-4 (cloth)
ISBN: 978-1-4985-9725-8 (pbk)
ISBN: 978-1-4985-9724-1 (electronic)

For Bernadette Gaudet (1910–1990), my mother

Contents

Acknowledgments ix

Introduction xi

PART I. THE PRE-CRITICAL PERIOD: A TIME OF EXPLORATION   1

1 Kant and the Optimism of Leibniz   3

2 The Origin and Nature of Evil   13

3 Is Philosophical Theodicy Possible for Kant?   33

PART II. THE EARLY CRITICAL PERIOD: A TIME OF TRANSITION   47

4 Setting the Scene   49

5 Aspects of Theodicy   59

6 Pulling the Strands Together   79

PART III. THE LATE-CRITICAL PERIOD: A TIME OF CONCLUSION   91

7 The Failure of Philosophical Theodicies   93

8 The Taxonomy of Evil Revisited   111

9 Kant's Own Authentic Theodicy   121

Conclusion	135
Bibliography	141
Index	145
About the Author	149

Acknowledgments

I wish to acknowledge the permissions given to use material from the following sources in this study: Cambridge University Press for the use of excerpts from Immanuel Kant's "Critique of Pure Reason," "Theoretical Philosophy, 1755–1770," and "Religion and Rational Theology" in The Cambridge Edition of the Works of Immanuel Kant, General Editors Paul Guyer and Allen Wood, Copyright © 1992 Cambridge University Press (reproduced with permission of the Licensor through PLSClear), De Gruyter, Berlin, for the inclusion of material from my contribution to the *Kant Yearbook 2018*, edited by D. H. Heidemann, and Professor Stephen Palmquist for allowing my use of his matrix presentation of the theodicies considered by Kant.

I wish to thank the editorial staff at Lexington Books with whom I have been working to produce this volume, in particular Jana Hodges-Kluck and Trevor Crowell. They have been an important source of help and encouragement in getting this far.

This study draws on both the philosophy of religion and Kant studies. I have been fortunate to have received generous assistance from experts in these fields, respectively Professor Maria Rosa Antognazza and Dr. John Callanan, both of King's College London. I have no doubt that they have materially aided this study, but whatever shortcomings it may still contain are to be laid at my door. Thanks are also owed to my daughter, Dr. Grace Huxford of Bristol University for her assiduous reading of various draft materials and her resultant suggestions. I also wish to thank Peter Byrne, Professor Emeritus of King's College, London who first directed my attention to the subject of theodicy in Kant's corpus. More important to the completion of my project than all my guides and helpers has been my wife Sarah. Her patience and support has been invaluable. There have been many evening mealtimes during which she has had to bear with my stumbling efforts to explain my work but any failure in that regard is again mine. However, I know that I have been successful in at least one regard as she is now firmly convinced of the validity and wisdom of the first formulation of Kant's Categorical Imperative.

To all, my thanks are due.

Introduction
Kant and Theodicy

The thesis which motivates and underpins this study is that Kant was engaged with the subject of theodicy throughout his career and not merely in his 1791 treatise explicitly devoted to the subject, *On the Failure of All Attempted Philosophical Theodicies.*[1] Accordingly, the study will trace his thought on this subject from early to late career to show not only the continuity of Kant's consideration but also his philosophical development on the subject.

The problem of evil, at its most simple, is the challenge to explain how it is possible that there is evil in a world created by an all-good, all-knowing, and all-powerful God. Whilst the problem of evil is usually couched and debated in Christian terms, it also confronts other religions. For example, in Islam, some of the ninety-nine names of Allah appear to conflict with the presence of evil in the world. Whilst theodicy, as the undertaking which attempts to find an answer to the problem of evil, has a long history *avant le mot*,[2] the word "theodicy" itself was introduced into the philosophical lexicon by G. W. Leibniz. Its etymology, a construction from the Greek words *Theos*—God and *dike*—justice, reveals Leibniz's intended answer. In his *Theodicy* of 1710, Leibniz specifically strove to link these two ideas and show that God's justice could be successfully defended in the face of evil in the world. In this way, Leibniz sought to defeat both the skepticism of Pierre Bayle and fideism. Leibniz's defense of God in this matter was grounded on the claim that our world is the best possible which God could have instantiated from all the possible worlds which He contemplated. This notion of the best possible world is more often known because of the withering scorn to which it was inaccurately[3] subjected in Voltaire's *Candide*.[4] The meaning assigned to "theodicy" still varies. For example the definition given in the *Oxford Dictionary of Philosophy*, namely "the part of theology concerned with defending the goodness and omnipotence of God in the face of evil and suffering in the world" (Blackburn, 2008, 361) without saying anything about the challenge evil presents to God's existence *per se*. Within the philosophy of religion, scholars still offer their own versions. One recent example comes from Peter Byrne (2007, 122) who sees theodicy as "a way of maintaining hope for the human good in the light of evil," a definition with overtones of self-deception which states what theodicy is *for* not what it *is*. That from Sam Duncan (2012, 974) tells us that a "theodicy needs only to give an account how evils in the world could bring about a good that justifies them," a definition that seems to confine theodicies to just those that offer an instrumental or greater good account of evil. These two definitions are also notable in that they do not contain any explicit reference to God.

However, as his thought on theodicy is the focus of this study, Kant's definition is the one on which to concentrate. At first sight, it seems to respond to a different concern than that of Leibniz, namely solely with God's justice:

> By "theodicy" we understand the defense of the highest wisdom of the creator against the charge which reason brings against it for whatever is counter-purposive in the word—We call this "the defending of God's cause." (*Failure*, 8:255)

Although Kant is not explicit in his definition regarding whose or what purpose is being countered, he soon makes it clear that he is considering the counter-purposiveness which "may be opposed to the wisdom of its [the world's] creator" (*Failure*, 8:256). In his definition, Kant envisages a broad scope for theodicy by his inclusion of "whatever." This has prompted Elhanan Yakira (2009, 148) to even suggest that Leibniz and Kant were indeed dealing with different questions on account of the different nature of evil being addressed. Whilst it has merit, Yakira's suggestion does not present a problem since, when *Failure* is examined, it will be seen that there are three types of counter-purposiveness considered: moral evil, physical evil, and injustice. As injustice concerns the relationship between the moral and the physical, I consider that Kant's definition of theodicy does not clash with that of Leibniz; it is just more comprehensive and explicit.

In my view, the word "reason" captures two distinct and significant meanings which cannot be readily divorced from each other. The first meaning has the sense of thinking, understanding, and forming judgments logically which could be grouped under the one term "reasoning." The second meaning has the sense of cause, explanation, or justification for an action or event. I contend that Kant's definition demands that both meanings are addressed in his theodicy. For Kant, unlike the fideist, a successful theodicy can only be established using reasoning. Nonetheless, it should still provide an explanation which reconciles the apparently irreconcilable, namely the counter-purposive and a theistic God. Thus the search for a theodicy is a search for an explanation which satisfies the demands of reason in the both senses described, in short, for a reasoned explanation.

Reason in its first meaning was supreme for Kant, not only in defining the limits of our possible knowledge, but also being the only foundation upon which to build a moral law that was not externally imposed but rather came from within. It is clear from his definition of theodicy that Kant holds that it is *reason* which brings the charge against God concerning counter-purposiveness. It also shows that the struggle between reason's demands and belief in a theistic God was a live issue for him. That throughout Kant's life there was tension between the unrelenting demands of reason (and his own in particular) and his striving to retain a place for God in his philosophical system is not a new topic in the literature. However, whilst other authors have highlighted such tension, none to date regard, as I do, Kant's career-long efforts to defuse it as an extended search for the reasoned explanation which would form an effective theodicy.

That for Kant there was tension between reason's demands and the notion of God should not be altogether surprising as one of the major undertakings and effects of the Enlightenment was to free humankind from the self-imposed tyranny of superstitious religion and give reason its head. Kant himself wrote in such terms in his 1784 essay *What is Enlightenment*? Some thinkers went to the opposite extreme from superstitious religion and denied God's existence *tout court*. There is abundant evidence that Kant was amongst those who could not or would not relinquish the notion of a deity who took a benevolent interest in Creation. I maintain that throughout his philosophical career, Kant retained a belief in God notwithstanding his aversion to organized religion. However, belief in God could never be allowed to undermine the primacy of reason. Strong evidence for this is that he continued to address the problems inherent in theodicy, construed as the reasoned explanation identified above. Nevertheless, it will be seen that what constituted a successful theodicy for Kant changed significantly as his career progressed. By 1791 he had concluded that all efforts to date to provide such a reasoned explanation were destined to fail when based on theoretical/speculative reason, in his terms, "philosophical" theodicy. If Kant was to maintain that theodicy *per se* was still possible an alternative route had to be found and he identified such a route in the treatise explicitly dealing with theodicy, *Failure*. Hence this study must also be concerned with the extent to which Kant's theodicy succeeded where he saw the efforts of others failing.

However, 1791 and *Failure* is not the time and place to begin any examination of Kant on theodicy. His considerations, which started as early as 1753 with his reflections on Leibniz's theodicy and the supposed theodicy of Alexander Pope in his *Essay on Man*, continued throughout his philosophical career. Indeed, he continued beyond the 1791 treatise to produce writings of theodical relevance, notably *Religion with the Boundaries of Mere Reason*.[5] The best evidence for Kant's concern with theodicy is the richness of primary sources containing material relevant to this study and this is illustrated in summary form in table 0.1. All of these sources must be leveraged if a comprehensive picture of the development over his philosophical career of Kant's thought on theodicy with all its twists and turns is to be understood.

It is not too soon to look at a potentially viable counter to my underpinning thesis. The counter would be to dispute my claim that Kant was engaged with theodicy throughout his career. The textual support which could be called upon for this counter would be that, in his total works, as presented in the *Akademie Ausgabe*, Kant uses the word *"Theodizee"* only nineteen times, twelve occurring in the single late-Critical work, *Failure*, whilst yet others refer to the title of Leibniz's work.[6] Moreover, a subsidiary counter argument is also available. This is that it is possible to regard the treatise specifically devoted to theodicy, *Failure*, merely as a device for attacking the then prevailing intellectual climate in the reign of Frederick William II of Prussia with its restrictions on theological and philosophical freedoms.[7] Dealing with this subsidiary counter first, I accept that Kant did use the treatise to criticize the political authorities. However, I will show in the main body of this study that this is not one of the treatise's more important aspects, these being (i) Kant's comparison of the types of counter-purposiveness with God's moral attributes and his subsequent evaluation of theodicies, (ii) the proposal of his own authentic theodicy, and (iii) his thought on sincerity which underlies authentic theodicy.

I hold that the principal counter is also defeasible. It is also best dealt with now before proceeding further as it touches on an important issue which supports many of the arguments which will be presented. The source of the defeat is to be found in Kant's definition of theodicy. In short, just as theodicy as an activity existed before the word, whenever Kant considered the nature and properties of God and those of evil with a view to reconciling them, he was engaged in theodicy even when not using the word. Now if Kant's thought on God and evil were static, we could just trace his developing thought on their relationship in the various theodicies which attempted to reconcile them. This would form an interesting enough account but Kant's thought on God and evil were far from static; significant developments took place in both areas. This meant that all changes in these two areas unavoidably had an impact on the work any putative theodicy had to do. When this is taken into account it will be immediately seen that the works listed in table 0.1 do indeed contain a wealth of material relevant to the purpose of this study. In other words, Kant's thought on theodicy must be set in the context

Table 0.1 Works of Importance to Theodicy

Date	Work	Period	Comment
1753–54	Reflections 3703–5	Pre-Critical	Kant reflects on Leibnizian theodicy and Pope's variant, favoring the latter. He raises two serious objections against that of Leibniz.
1755	Universal Natural History	Pre-Critical	Kant introduces the idea of universal laws of nature and their uninterrupted working. He endorses a Newtonian view of the physical world.
1755	A New Elucidation of the First Principles of Metaphysical Cognition	Pre-Critical	Having again considered the notion of a Best Possible World, Kant examines whether human beings are free and God's responsibility (or not) for evil.
1756	The 3 Earthquake Essays	Pre-Critical	Kant responds to the Lisbon earthquake (1755), claiming physical evil does not result from moral evil and is not divine punishment.
1759	An Attempt at Some Reflections on Optimism	Pre-Critical	Kant mounts a stout metaphysical defense of the concept of the Best Possible World and God's choice thereof.
1763	The Only Possible Argument in Support of a Demonstration of the Existence of God	Pre-Critical	Whilst in no way doubting God's existence, Kant registers dissatisfaction with metaphysical proofs of it. This threatens Leibnizian theodicy.
1763	Attempt to Introduce the Concept of Negative Magnitudes in Philosophy	Pre-Critical	Kant challenges the notion of evil conceived solely as limitation. He sees evil also as something negative with a positive ground and thus opposing the good. Evil is not only an absence. He makes an important differentiation between *mala defectus* and *mala privationis*.
1781	Critique of Pure Reason (First Edition)	Early-Critical	Kant shows that we are unable to have knowledge of God via theoretical reason. He also dismisses the three traditional proofs for God's existence. This will debar any theodicy based on such knowledge or proofs.

(Continued)

Table 0.1 **Works of Importance to Theodicy** (continued)

Date	Work	Period	Comment
1783–84	Lectures on the Philosophical Doctrine of Religion	Early-Critical	Kant retains some aspects of Leibnizian theodicy, rejects others, and introduces some aspects which he will elaborate in later works.
1784	Idea for a Universal History with a Cosmopolitan Aim	Early-Critical	Kant further considers aspects of theodicy raised in Lectures.
1786	Conjectural Beginning of Human History	Early-Critical	Kant deals with aspects of theodicy as reported in Lectures.
1788	Critique of Practical Reason	Late-Critical	Kant argues for immortality and God as postulates of pure practical reason based on the Highest Good, thus advancing a moral faith.
1790	Critique of the Power of Judgment	Late-Critical	Kant advances a moral telos for humankind, the Highest Good, and discusses further the moral deity and moral faith.
1791	On the Failure of All Attempted Philosophical Theodicies	Late-Critical	Kant dismisses all philosophical theodicies but advances his own "authentic" theodicy based on moral faith which in turn is based on practical reason as advanced in the second Critique.
1793	Religion within the Boundaries of Mere Reason	Late-Critical	Kant unequivocally assigns responsibility for evil to man which appears to free God from the responsibility, thus providing a theodicy.
1794	The End of All Things	Late-Critical	Kant asserts the impossibility of change in the non-temporal, intelligible world.

of his developing thought on God and evil. In this way, it is intimately related to Kant's overall treatment of these two subjects, which few would argue were not ever-present concerns in his philosophy. This view is supported by Yakira, who states that "from the Leibnizian Considerations on optimism of 1759, up to the anti-Leibnizian texts *On the failure of all the attempts to answer philosophical questions in regard to theodicy* of 1791[8] and *On the radical evil in human nature* of 1792,[9] Kant returns again and again to this issue [evil]" (2009, 154). Nevertheless, the study cannot and will not attempt to offer a complete account of Kant on evil or on God. A full treatment of either subject on its own would not only deviate from the mainline of this study but also greatly exceed the scope available to it. Illustrating this, in his authoritative *Kant Dictionary*, Howard Caygill states in the entry on "God," that "a comprehensive account of the entirety of Kant's view on God . . . is still awaited" (1995, 215). If Caygill's claim is still correct[10] and over two hundred years of Kant scholarship has not yet achieved this objective, then my aim here must be more modest. Thus the study will only focus on those aspects of these two extensive subjects, god and evil, which interact with each other, actually or potentially, in the context of theodicy.

Some more general introductory remarks are also in order. To find a successful theodicy is only a challenge for those who believe in God or want a place for Him in their philosophical system. Showing Kant was concerned with theodicy throughout his career provides evidence that Kant did indeed strive to retain a place for God in his system and that his struggle to reconcile a belief in God with reason's demands regarding evil was real and ongoing. I consider that it is fair to regard this struggle not as an abstract one for Kant but as personal since he was to the fore in his time in the effort to define reason's power and limitations. In addition, if evil can be fully explained away or dismissed then there is equally no need for theodicy as the reconciliation of evil with God's moral attributes and I believe Kant was equally aware of this. In short, the existence of both God and evil must be live propositions for anyone concerned with theodicy. If either is missing, the whole subject becomes moot.

It is also useful to position the study about to be undertaken in the context of Kantian scholarship. A significant motivation for studying the scope and development of Kant's theodicy is that it is a topic rarely considered by Kant scholars, a notable exception being A. L. Loades' excellent *Kant and Job's Comforters* (1985). Also, as the study is concerned with the whole of Kant's career, it will necessarily encompass his pre-Critical period, again a relatively lightly studied area.[11] The combined effect of subject and time-period, both lightly studied, means there are relatively few secondary sources to inform an examination of Kant's thought on theodicy in this period. The tenor of this part of the study will thus be one of exploration, seeking to identify the thematic development in the primary material. This situation changes significantly with respect to his Critical period, both early and late. There, papers devoted to Kantian theodicy are available, albeit still in relatively limited numbers when compared to other aspects of his philosophy. But, given that the study's scope must include the changes in Kant's stance on God and evil, there is abundant material, particularly on the controversial issue of the Highest Good. Here the emphasis will be less on identifying what Kant said but rather on looking at it afresh in the light of his concern with theodicy. It is my aim to view Kant's Critical period in a theodical light whilst taking care not to introduce any distortions by forcing the reader to interpret it through the lens of theodicy. The subject of Kantian theodicy has received a timely and welcome boost with two recent papers, Sam Duncan's "Moral Evil, Freedom and the Goodness of God:

Why Kant abandoned Theodicy" (2012), and "Kant's Kritik der Theodizee—Eine Metakritik" by Hubertus Busche (2013). Whilst I differ from them in key areas it is my hope that, through this study, I will be able to contribute to the debate on Kant and theodicy which has been re-enlivened by their valuable contributions. Also in the same spirit in which Kant presented *Only Possible Argument*, I hope that others will find some materials of use in this study on which to build further, perhaps in resolving those issues identified in this study which arise from Kant's occasional ambivalence.

Additionally, theodicy can be seen as one of those subjects which performs a unifying and integrating function in Kant's thought, because his consideration of the subject draws on his moral philosophy, his philosophy of religion, and, at times, his philosophy of history. Approaching Kant through theodicy thus provides an innovative interpretative route. The benefits of taking this less trodden route into Kant's philosophy will be seen from the richness of issues uncovered by doing so. These are set out in summary below in the form of the main and subsidiary theses for which I will be arguing, together with some important qualifications.

MAIN THESES

In the course of this study I will advance the following major theses.

(a) The first and all-encompassing one is that that Kant had a career-long concern with theodicy (contra Loades), where theodicy is construed as above, and that his concern is not confined to *Failure*. According to this thesis, whenever Kant is engaged in a rational reconciliation between evil and God, I maintain that he is, in essence and effect, engaged in theodicy. His efforts to find such reconciliation represent a career-long search for an effective theodicy which in turn can be seen as part of his continuing efforts to find and/or retain a place for God in his philosophical system.

(b) Kant's stance on what constituted a successful theodicy developed through his career starting, in his pre-Critical Period, from the datum provided by Leibniz's theodicy. In the early part of his Critical period, Kant did not have a clear position on theodicy but later he established his substantive position in advancing his own, "authentic," theodicy. This authentic theodicy marked a discontinuity in his thinking and was grounded in moral faith based on *practical* reason, not on simple fideism which he rejected. In his pre-Critical and early-Critical periods, Kant had accepted philosophical theodicies but with *Failure* he no longer did so.

(c) This follows from (b). Kant did not reject *all* theodicies (contra Duncan). However, he did indeed reject all *philosophical* theodicies in *Failure*. The use by Kant of the word "philosophical" in connection with theodicies requires clarification. For him, these theodicies are based upon *theoretical, speculative*, reason. Additionally, he later also terms such theodicies "doctrinal." Further, given this special, technical, use of "philosophical," it would be an unwarranted inference that his "authentic" theodicy was therefore in any way non-philosophical where "philosophical" is given its usual, broader reading.

(d) The cumulative effect of Kant's consideration of natural science and his Critical epistemology acted to constrain his own eventual theodicy. The former constraint limits the evil required to be reconciled within a theodicy. The latter constraint forces the would-be theodicy constructor to seek another route to God which does not amount to a knowledge claim and yet provides a robust enough foundation upon which to base a theodicy.

(e) Metaphysical evil conceived as limitation in Leibniz's taxonomy of evil performs the same function as Kant's late-Critical radical evil, namely providing the ground for the possibility of moral evil, rather than being evil *per se*.

(f) The thesis with which the study culminates is that Kant's own, authentic, theodicy fails because it does not meet Kant's own definition of theodicy. However, this failure does not imply that Kant was not therefore concerned with theodicy throughout his career. His sincere efforts, based on his moral system grounded in *practical* reason, can still be correctly termed an attempted *reasoned* explanation of how the apparently irreconcilable, God and evil, can be reconciled.

SUBSIDIARY THESES

There are byproducts still worthy of note which emerge from the work to establish the main theses. The first is that Kant changed his stance on evil as a limitation in 1763 with *Negative Magnitudes* not in 1790 as a result of the work of C. C. E. Schmid (contra Duncan). The second is that Kant's rejection of philosophical theodicies is sound, as it is ultimately based on the epistemological boundaries established in the first *Critique*. This differs from the approach of Busche who concentrates on assessing the soundness of the individual arguments which Kant uses to reject the evaluated theodicies in *Failure*. Although Busche makes some compelling criticisms of Kant's individual arguments, the overall effect is to downplay Kant's rejection of philosophical theodicies *per se*. Finally, since Kant rejects philosophical theodicies on principle, I will claim that his rejection is more comprehensive than rejection of those arguments based on moral evil (contra Duncan).

The study has three main parts, each of which covers one of the time periods into which Kant's career was divided in table 0.1.

Part I. The Pre-Critical Period

As stated earlier, I characterize the period as exploratory on Kant's part. We should not, however, expect a smooth, linear, progression in his thought or consistency in this period.[12] This will be clearly seen in the detailed examination. Nevertheless, the period was still one in which Kant reached definitive positions on certain aspects of theodicy that were retained by him through his whole career. The first of these is that he embraced the idea of a physical world governed by universal laws of nature as described by Newton whilst still retaining a place for God in his philosophical system. Second, Kant came to see the harm done in nature not as evil despite any unfortunate effects on human beings and certainly not as the punishment for the moral evil which humans commit. Third, I will argue that it was in this period that Kant first provided strong evidence of moving from accepting evil as only resulting from limitation to a position where he additionally saw it as something ontologically positive. These three aspects will be discussed in chapter 2. Other topics on which Kant did not reach a conclusive result included necessitation as opposed to freedom, and the possibility of a successful theoretical proof for God's existence. All these topics deserve detailed attention because of the material they contain bears directly on the job that any would-be theodicy is asked to do. However, before proceeding to this, it is important to recognize that any discussion of theodicy during Kant's pre-Critical period must always be set in the context provided by Leibniz's *Theodicy* of 1710. Thus it is with this topic that the detailed examination starts in chapter 1. Part I concludes with chapter 3 where the question is examined whether philosophical theodicies as characterized by Kant were possible for him in this pre-Critical period.

Part II. The Early-Critical Period

Treatment of this period is an essential bridging element in this study as it is not sufficient to merely contrast the pre-Critical starting point of Kant's theodical journey with his eventual late-Critical destination. In examining this period, I am differing from the approach of Loades (cf. 1985, 76) who considers that theodicy or optimism was a subject only taken up by Kant in early and late career. In contrast, I hold that (i) Kant's consideration of theodicy continued through mid-career and (ii) that the early-Critical period offers the scholar much in the way of explanation of his late career stance. "Transition" fits well with this period because it conveys a sense of moving, modification, evolution, and indeed change but without this being abrupt, discontinuous, or revolutionary. There are topics, significant for theodicy, where Kant's views are continuous with, or unchanged from, his pre-Critical period and topics where there was indeed a clear change of mind. Also, there are topics which can be described as innovations in the sense that they are appearing in his thoughts for the first time but not yet taking the definitive form adopted in his late-Critical period. It is the presence and nature of these three categories which provide good reason for viewing this period as transitional. I will argue that, whilst the period is transitional for Kant on theodicy, it is one which nevertheless ends with significant unresolved tensions in his views on the subject. Chapter 4 deals with two important preliminaries (i) justifying reliance on the *Lectures on the Philosophical Doctrine of Religion*,[13] which recorded lectures given in 1783/1784 and (ii) investigating the impact of the first *Critique* on theodicy *überhaupt*. Then, in chapter 5, the various topics, collected into the three groups unchanged, changed, and innovations, are considered together with the implications for any possible theodicy. In this part's final chapter, 6, whether philosophical theodicy is possible for Kant will be re-examined before lastly considering the tensions which remain unresolved at the end of the period due to Kant's epistemology running ahead of his thought on theodicy.

Part III. The Late-Critical Period

Kant's change of stance on theodicy was not coincident with the famous Copernican turn in his metaphysics and epistemology, a view supported by Christophe Schulte (1991, 372) and Duncan (2012, 974) amongst others. His theodical thought lagged behind. In the late-Critical period, theodicy caught up when Kant adopted his authoritative stance on the subject. This did not occur in an incremental fashion, resolving the individual tensions to be described in Part II but with a single step, his 1791 treatise *Failure*. In Part III, we will adopt Kant's *modus operandi* and move directly to consideration of *Failure* where Kant had two principal aims, one negative and the other positive.

His negative aim is to dismiss all philosophical theodicies and this is considered in chapter 7. This is a fundamental change from his early-Critical period when Kant still saw such theodicies as possible. Both Kant's method of working and the arguments put forward in *Failure* will be examined in order to test his claim. One issue which he deals with in rejecting philosophical theodicies is the perennial one of evil as limitation, so the evaluation of his negative aim will be followed by revisiting his taxonomy of evil. This will be first treated in Part I of the study, Kant's pre-Critical period, but Part III explores whether his thought on evil can be brought into a final unified form. In chapter 8, I argue that it can.

As Kant did not reject *all* theodicies, his positive aim in *Failure*, namely to advance his own "authentic" theodicy, is then explored in chapter 9.

A subsidiary objective was to use the work to obliquely attack the atmosphere of intellectual-theological censorship which existed in Prussia at the time of its writing. At first glance, this might seem irrelevant to theodicy were it not for the fact that Kant was concerned not only with intellectual freedom but also with honesty and sincerity. These will be seen to be key components of his "authentic" theodicy. Since Kant shows to his satisfaction that all philosophical theodicies fail, we must ask whether his own theodicy fares any better. The outcome of this is that, in chapter 9, I argue for the failure of authentic theodicy because it does not meet Kant's own definition of theodicy.

I conclude the study by summarizing the results and outlining some of the implications for moral faith and theodicy. And so, *ad fontes*.

NOTES

1. Hereafter *Failure*. This title is the one adopted by Michel Despland for his translation of *Über das Mißlingen aller philosophischen Versuche in der Theodizee*. It has been used in this study rather than the more usual *On the Miscarriage of all Philosophical Trials in Theodicy* because, in my view, the word "Miscarriage" is capable of sending the wrong signal. "Miscarriage" commonly suggests a legal process which has resulted in the wrong verdict. Significantly, it will be seen that at no point in *Failure* does Kant advance the notion that God has been falsely found innocent or guilty on the charge that He has allowed evil in the world; in other words, no verdict is pronounced. Also "failure" is more indicative of what goes wrong with the theodicies which Kant considers.

2. For example, see Nadler (2008) for an account of theodicy in Jewish thought before Leibniz.

3. Voltaire's attack was based on *a posteriori* cases of evil in the world; Leibniz's theodicy is an *a priori* argument.

4. Murray and Greenberg (2013) note that "Leibniz's approach to the problem of evil became known to many readers through Voltaire's lampoon in *Candide*: the link that Voltaire seems to forge between Leibniz and the extravagant optimism of Dr. Pangloss continues—for better or worse—to shape the popular understanding of Leibniz's approach to the problem of evil."

5. Hereafter, *Religion*.

6. Whilst this excludes references to "optimism," which in the pre-Critical period was largely synonymous with "theodicy," this only adds another three references to the count.

7. Beiser (1987, 118) highlights Kant's concern as expressed in *Was heißt: Sich im Denken orientieren* (8:114).

8. *Failure*.

9. The first part of *Religion*.

10. Peter Byrne's *Kant on God* (2007) is directed at this lacuna.

11. Martin Schönfeld (2000, 6, also 248n3) has examined the incidence of articles on the pre-Critical period and found that of the 500 approximate articles on Kant, which have appeared in the *Kant-Studien* of the last sixty years, less than two dozen concern his pre-Critical philosophy.

12. Indeed Cassirer (1908, 92–94) considers that the whole of Kant's career was typified by erratic progress toward its goals.

13. Hereafter *Lectures*.

Part I

THE PRE-CRITICAL PERIOD
A Time Of Exploration

INTRODUCTORY REMARKS

This first period was one of exploration into theodicy for Kant in which he examined existing theodicies against the backdrop provided by that of Leibniz. He also identified the first constraints which later help define the available scope for his own theodicy. At times, as befits a time of exploration, Kant appears to change his mind and offer perspectives that do not always cohere with earlier views. But it would be uncharitable to insist on coherence at a time when Kant was making the first efforts to formulate his position on theodicy and its components. The themes to be examined, in addition to his stance on aspects of Leibniz's theodicy, will include how Kant endorses a Newtonian worldview in which the laws of nature are ubiquitous and unchanging, his thoughts on necessitation and freedom, and his evolving views on the origin and nature of evil. Attention to the last mentioned is particularly important because, in order to assess Kant's theodical thought, it must be established what he regarded as evil and what not.

Chapter 1

Kant and the Optimism of Leibniz

A prominent example of Kant not always steering a steady course in his pre-Critical exploration of theodicy is his attitude toward that of Leibniz. Although there are some references to Leibniz's system in other pre-Critical works, Kant provides two main sources of evidence on this subject. The first are the Reflections 3703–5 from 1753 to 1754. These were most likely his notes for a possible entry in the prize-essay announced by the Prussian Royal Academy in 1753 for its 1755 prize essay competition with the optimism of Alexander Pope as contained in his *Essay on Man* as its subject. The competition was designed by Maupertuis as an indirect attack on the optimism of Leibniz by inviting respondents to compare the systems of Pope and Leibniz. Kant's notes thus contain comment on both.[1] The second is his *Attempt at Some Reflections on Optimism*[2] from just five years later in 1759. The problem and challenge for the Kant scholar is that they are radically different both in tone and content. The Reflections relate Kant's understanding of Leibnizian theodicy and offer a comparison by him with the supposed system of Alexander Pope in his *Essay on Man* (1734). In addition, in Reflection 3705, Kant also tables two non-trivial criticisms of Leibniz's system. *Optimism*, on the other hand, is a ringing endorsement of the key aspect of Leibnizian theodicy, that of the best possible world. However, any attempt to relate the two texts to each other and search for their possible reconciliation can only follow a closer look at both sources starting with the Reflections.

It is in Reflection 3704 that Kant starts his consideration of Leibnizian optimism (theodicy)[3] with: "optimism is the doctrine which justifies the existence of evil in the world by assuming that there is an infinitely perfect, benevolent and omnipotent original Being" (*Refl*, 17:230). This is best read as optimism being the attempt to justify the presence of evil *despite* there being an infinitely perfect, benevolent and omnipotent original Being. In my reading of this, there is also a suggestion that Kant did not differentiate between assuming that God exists and relying on an antecedent proof of God's existence as Leibniz does.[4] There is, of course, a clear difference in the robustness of these two cases. However, Kant further shows his clear understanding of the Leibnizian system which encompasses the crucial notion of the best possible world when he states that "this justification is . . . that, in spite of all the apparent contradictions that which is chosen by this infinitely perfect Being, must nonetheless be the best of all that is possible" (*Refl*, 17:231). This could also suggest that God could only choose the best because it is God who is doing the choosing, an idea to which we will return when examining *Optimism* in detail. Kant also highlights another key aspect of Leibnizian theodicy, namely the differentiation between God's *antecedent* and the *consequent* will (cf. *Refl*, 17:231). The former means that God wills no evil *per se*, but the act of Creation unavoidably involves creating beings with limitations which are the condition of the possibility of evil. Thus, God only allows or permits evil consequent upon creation without wanting evil *per se*. Leibniz had expressed this as:

> Hence the conclusion that God wills all good *in himself antecedently*, that he wills the best *consequently* as an *end*, that he wills what is indifferent, and physical evil, sometimes as a *means*, but that he will only permit moral evil as the *sine quo non* or as a hypothetical necessity which connects it with the best. Therefore the *consequent will* of God which has sin for its object, is only *permissive*. (§25/H138)[5]

Kant confirms his understanding of the importance of the concept of antecedent and consequent wills to Leibniz's system at *Refl* 17:231. Leibniz's taxonomy of evil from which Kant provides no evidence of disagreement in the Reflections under consideration runs as follows:

> Evil may be taken metaphysically, physically and morally. *Metaphysical evil* consists in mere imperfection, *physical evil* in suffering and *moral evil* in sin. Now although physical evil and moral evil are not necessary, it is enough that by virtue of the eternal verities they may be possible. (§21/H136)

Here metaphysical evil arises from Creation's finitude which means that it must necessarily fall short of the Creator's perfection. The other two types of evil, Kant describes as "those which are contingent, and are either hypothetical and physical or hypothetical and moral" (*Refl*, 17:231). Here, it is important to recognize the connection which Leibniz sees between moral and physical evil:

It is therefore not God who is the cause of moral evil: but he is the cause of physical evil, that is, the punishment of moral evil. And this punishment, far from being incompatible with the supremely good principle, of necessity emanates from that one of its attributes . . . justice, which is not less essential to it than its goodness. (§155/H220)

Leibniz could not be clearer; physical evil is punishment for moral evil. For him, this is consistent with God as a just judge. This link between moral and physical evil is another important element in Leibniz's theodicy but one, looking forward, Kant will reject as early as 1755 in *Universal Natural History*. Kant does not reconsider this rejection at any point later in his philosophical career; indeed, he endorses it explicitly at various points including the earthquake essays of 1756. The above citation also suggests that Leibniz sees justice being dispensed in this world and not, unlike Kant, finally achieved in the next. Notwithstanding that, Leibniz prefigures Kant in acknowledging that physical evil/well-being is not always distributed in proper proportion to moral evil/virtue (cf. §43/H98). This imbalance[6] is a central concern for Kant throughout his philosophical career. Later, it drives a major innovation in his moral philosophy which underpins his own eventual "authentic" theodicy. The innovation in question is the Highest Good.

Another important aspect of Kant's understanding of Leibniz's optimism is shown by the following:

God's wisdom and goodness nonetheless turns them [the permitted evils as a result of Creation] to the advantage of the whole, so that the displeasure they arouse when viewed in isolation is completely outweighed in the whole by the compensation which the divine goodness is able to institute. (*Refl*, 17:231)

Two important aspects stand out here. First, both passages suggest that Kant's understanding of Leibniz's theodicy is what could be termed a "Net Good Theodicy," which regards the presence of a particular evil as justified on the basis that the harm it does is outweighed by the good that the evil produces. Should that be what Kant understood at the time, he was mistaken. Leibniz was quite clear at several points in his *Theodicy* that he was not seeking to defend individual evils. This was the same misapprehension which Voltaire was under in *Candide*. Should Leibniz have been arguing in such a manner it would have been *a posteriori*. However, this is not the nature of Leibniz's theodicy which is an *a priori* argument in which he is concerned with the goodness of Creation as a whole. He argues that there is no way that we can know that removing a particular moral evil would create a better whole, stating, "Thus one can esteem fittingly the good things done by God only when one considers their whole extent by relating them to the entire universe" (§119/H191), but we simply do not have such a universal view (cf. §211–14/H260–62). Further, just as Kant and Pope will do later, Leibniz considers that the good in the world is not to be assessed solely from a human standpoint or even that of rational creatures in general.

Second, it can also be noted that Kant does not question God's goodness, wisdom, or power, regarding them as "sufficiently well-known from other indisputable reasons" (*Refl*, 17:232). Unfortunately, Kant does not set out these reasons or their source. From such we would know whether Kant was relying upon a theoretical proof of God's existence or was just assenting to those attributes normally assigned to a theistic God in the mid-eighteenth century. The citation also suggests a "Limited View Theodicy" where our judgment of our world as sub-optimal results from our inability to see the whole of God's Creation. We have seen above that Leibniz would have approved of this aspect of Kant's understanding. Kant provided his final verdict on these two theodicy types in his late-Critical period when they were among the variants considered and rejected by him in *Failure*.

Unsurprisingly, these Reflections also contain material on Pope's *Essay* since the Prussian Royal Academy prize essay question for 1755 specifically requested a comparison of the optimistic systems of Leibniz and Pope. Holding the latter's to be superior, Kant identifies a key difference in his view between them being that Leibniz regarded the perceived imperfections in the world as real (cf. *Refl*, 17:233). This contrasts with Pope who states at several points in the *Essay* "whatever is, is right" (1/10,[7] 4/5, 7). This implies that Pope does not admit defects; they are only apparent. However if such a construct is to work and is to consider all evil that is in the world, moral evil must also fall under "whatever is, is right." When one examines the *Essay*, it is clear that Pope at least is definitely prepared to consider the possibility of moral evil also resulting from fixed laws of nature:

- If plagues or earthquakes break not Heaven's design,
- Why then a Borgia, or a Cataline? (I/5)[8]

And

- From pride, from pride, our very reas'ning springs;
- Account for moral as for natural things:
- Why charge we Heaven in those, in these acquit?
- In both, to reason right, is to submit. (I/5)

In these two citations Pope also does not accept physical evil as evil, where physical evil is taken as the harmful results of the ubiquitous and unchanging laws of nature. Clearly, Pope's view that *all* apparent evils are just the results of the laws of nature would mean that we are necessitated in our moral behavior. Should that be the case, there would be no moral evil *per se* since responsibility for (im)moral actions could then not be assigned to human beings. In such circumstances there would be no job for theodicy left to do. There is, however, no indication in Kant's writings that he accepted or even entertained the idea that moral evil was the unavoidable consequence of laws of nature. This is just as well as any defender of God's goodness and justice would have an uphill task to show how God was not responsible for moral evil in choosing to instantiate a possible world where this was unavoidable as result of some law outside man's control. Nevertheless, Kant's notes show that he fully understood the impact of Pope's stance with the following in which he makes no exception of moral evil: "Pope subjects the creation to detailed scrutiny, particularly where it most seems to lack harmony; and yet he shows that each thing, which we might wish to see removed from the scheme of greatest perfection, is also, when considered in itself, good" (*Refl*, 17:233). To my mind, what is prompting Kant's thought here are the nature and limits of compossibility—how things, good when considered individually, when combined do not also produce good. Kant revisits the issue in Reflection 3705 which opens with an accurate summary of Leibniz's system. However, Kant immediately follows this by explicitly rejecting the Leibnizian system stating that it contains serious errors. He signals two such errors, the first concerning compossibility, identifying the kernel of this error as:

> What is it which causes the essential determinations of things to conflict with each other when combined . . . so that the perfections, each of which would increase God's pleasure, become incompatible? What is the nature of the unfathomable conflict which exists between the general will of God . . . and the metaphysical necessity which is not willing to adapt itself to that end in a general harmony which knows no exceptions? (*Refl*, 17:236)

In other words, Kant believes he has identified a metaphysical necessity to which even God's intentions must yield and it is this, not God, which results in things which are perfect in isolation becoming imperfect in combination. Additionally, should that be the case, this metaphysical necessity must be outside God, so undermining His omnipotence and any notion that He encompasses all reality. Susan Neiman supports such an interpretation. She states that "his [Leibniz's] defense of God argued that God could not have done any better than He did. But every lawyer has his price. In the process of defending God, Leibniz disempowered Him" (2002, 26). This is serious when one recalls that, in Kant's view, Leibniz's optimism assumes an omnipotent original Being (cf. *Refl*, 17:230). Kant reflects further on why one good combined with another can result in something less than good and eventually reaches the conclusion that the mistake consists in the fact that Leibniz identifies the scheme of the best world on the one hand with a kind of independence, and on the other with a dependence on the will of God (cf. *Refl*, 17:237). The two horns of the apparent dilemma are (i) the independence from God resulting from the metaphysical necessity (cf. *Refl*, 17:236) which prevents two perfections being perfect in combination and (ii) the dependence on the will of God comes from the notion that all is from God. In my view, the dilemma is only resolved when, in effect, Kant embraces *both* horns in two works from 1763. First, in Kant's *Only Possible Argument in Support of a Demonstration of the Existence of God*,[9] God is recognized as source of everything which is possible. Second, in *Negative Magnitudes*, Kant recognizes that non-compossibility when arises two entities have logically conflicting attributes (*NM*, 2:171) and even God cannot alter this. However, that eventual resolution does not affect what is at issue here in 1753/1754, his problem with Leibniz's system of optimism containing this apparent impasse of compossibility.

In Kant's eyes, the second error in the Leibnizian system is no less serious and his exposition of the problem cannot be improved upon:

> The second . . . mistake of optimism consists in the fact that the evils...which are perceived in the world are only excused on the assumption God exists; the mistake consists, therefore, in having first to believe that an . . . Infinitely Perfect Being exists, before one can be assured that the world . . . is beautiful and regular, instead of believing that the universal agreement of the arrangements of the world . . . itself furnishes the most beautiful proof of the existence of God. The most reliable and easiest proof therefore, of the reality of [God] . . . is undermined by Leibniz's system. (*Refl*, 17:238)

However, it is still useful to note two points. The first is perhaps so self-evident that it could be easily ignored. Without a *Theos*, there is no theodicy. The second is the status of the *Theos*; has its existence been the subject of an antecedent proof, or is it the object of a belief? For Leibniz it is the first case, but here Kant seems to be associating himself with the second. In turn, this gives rise to the serious error which Kant sees, namely, that if one starts from only a belief that God exists, one can indeed argue that the evils which result from *disorders* in the world are unavoidable for God in Creation. However, given the disorder in the world which evil represents, one cannot simultaneously reverse the argument and argue from the perceived *order* in the world to God's existence. A cannot call on B as proof in an argument at the same time as B is calling on A. The result would be a "deadly embrace" with no result. It is this which Kant argues undermines Leibniz's system, or as Robert Theis puts it: "at the end of the day, the metaphysico-theological project of Leibniz lacks unity" (2009, 161), holding that Kant saw that there was no connection of Leibniz's proof of God's existence in the *Monadology* and his notion of the best possible world. However, it is only the proof from order in the world, the Physico-Theological proof, which is here undermined; the other two main proofs, the Ontological and the Cosmological, are not affected. Kant will eventually address this second error through not accepting but rather deconstructing the problem. In the first *Critique* all theoretical proofs of God's existence, including the Physico-Theological, will be explicitly rejected with the result that it loses its power to undermine anything. However, in the first *Critique*, Kant remains attracted to the Physico-Theological proof (A623f/B651f) but then chiefly as an explanatory mechanism for the order in nature. Nevertheless, in the work under immediate consideration, Kant provides early indications of his concern for theodicy's success being predicated on any theoretical proof of God's existence.

> Thus, the properties of God are placed in safety to the satisfaction of those who have enough understanding and sufficient submissiveness to applaud the metaphysical proofs of the Divine Existence. As for the rest of those who are willing to acknowledge that contemplating the world reveals traces of God—they remain troubled. (*Refl*, 17:233)

It is reasonable to place Kant amongst the troubled despite him stating that "contemplating the world reveals traces of God." Even so, at this stage in his philosophical career, Kant approves one proof, that of Pope. He states that "Pope chooses a path which, when it comes to rendering the beautiful proof of God's existence accessible to everyone, is the best suited of all possible paths" (*Refl*, 17:233). However, to my reading, in Pope's *Essay* there is no explicit proof of God's existence but rather intimation that people come to God through Nature which is not dissimilar to the Physico-Theological proof that Kant regarded as undermined by Leibniz's best possible world.

If this was the only evidence available with which to assess Kant's stance on Leibniz's optimism, it would be reasonable to conclude that he firmly rejected it. However, the contrast with *Optimism* could not be more striking. The prevailing view expressed in the secondary literature concerning *Optimism* is that Kant is setting out a defense of the Leibnizian best possible world. For instance, Josef Kremer (1909, 161) holds that in the work "Kant is still a supporter of the Leibnizian optimism and defends the teaching of God's choice of the best possible world from among those possible."[10] Loades (1985, 110) concurs considering the work to be "an unambiguous reaffirmation of Leibniz." She adds that "Kant seems by now to have chosen to rely entirely on Leibniz and largely to have abandoned allusions to Pope" because any value the latter might have depended on the former.

In *Optimism* Kant demonstrates to his satisfaction, carefully and at some length, three crucial propositions which are contained in the Leibnizian position on the best possible world:

i. That there is a singular best possible world;
ii. That God would, acting from his nature, choose such a world; and
iii. That our world is this best possible world.

However, one important reservation must be noted. Kant starts his essay with the phrase "[n]ow that an appropriate concept of God has been formed, if God chooses, he chooses only what is best" (*Opt*, 2:29). But he does not describe this concept or state whether the concept is the subject of proof, belief, or just the opening premise of an argument. There is no doubt that *Optimism* proceeds from some prior stance on God's existence and is thus unchanged from the Reflections where Kant was equally unforthcoming on the subject of God's attributes. The second element of the citation concerning God's choice is also revealing as it shows that, here at least, part of the concept <God> is such a being chooses the best. This is strongly suggested by the following dismissive statement: "if anybody were so bold as to assert that the Supreme Wisdom could find the worse better than the best, or that the Supreme Goodness should prefer a lesser good to a greater. . . . I should not waste my time in attempting a refutation" (*Opt*, 2:33). The key weakness of the argumentation here, to my mind, is the premise above in which God is defined as, rather than shown to be, the type of entity that always chooses the best. This begs the question and leaves any theodicy based on this argument on insecure foundations.

One should also note that Kant viewed Leibniz as believing that he had said nothing original "when he [Leibniz] maintained that this world was the best of all possible worlds" (*Opt*, 2:29). For Kant, what was new was Leibniz's using that principle to "cut the knot, so difficult to untie, of all the difficulties relating to the origin of evil" (ibid.). In other words, Leibniz was employing the principle of the best possible world[11] to address what is now termed the logical problem of evil.[12] These reservations notwithstanding, there can be little doubt that in *Optimism* Kant is endorsing the Leibnizian system, from both a philosophical standpoint and a personal one. This can be seen from those passages, already cited and in the continuation of *Opt*, 2:34, in which Kant states that he is "happy to find myself a citizen of the world which could not possibly have been better than it is."

The challenge arising from the Reflections and *Optimism* is how can they be at all reconciled, between a rejection in 1754 and an endorsement just five years later? In my view, they cannot be. But, with the leeway allowed to

Kant in this exploratory period, one should not be overly concerned; a charge of inconsistency would be premature and certainly out of place. However, I consider that there are various arguments which can be presented in an effort to narrow but not eliminate the divide between the two sources.

First, we have noted that the two serious problems which Kant signaled in Reflection 3705 were rendered harmless by later development in his thought. However, even after making backdated allowance for this, at the time of the Reflections, Kant's position is a long way from an endorsement of Leibnizian theodicy. Second, when we look at the three propositions which Kant holds that he demonstrated in *Optimism*, one could argue that all he has endorsed is the Best Possible World, not a theodicy based on it. As noted, what Kant regarded as new with Leibniz was not the Best Possible World *per se* but its use to defend God's justice through his theodicy.

However, this is not enough for us to proceed to other topics. We must also look at how Kant viewed *Optimism* later in his career since we are concerned with the *development* of Kant's thought on theodicy. It would seem that Kant was embarrassed by *Optimism*. David Walford in his introduction to his translation of *Optimism* being used in this study cites Borowski, Kant's earliest biographer, as stating when he [Borowski] had enquired about the work:

> Kant, with genuine solemn seriousness bade me think no more on optimism, urging me, should I ever come across it anywhere, not to let anyone have a copy but to withdraw it from circulation immediately. (2002, lvi)

Borowski's testimony is important as his biography was read in sketch form by Kant, corrected in places by him, and approved in general (Kuehn, 2001, 10). This occurred in 1792 during the productive period some twelve years before Kant's death and so well before the period in which some scholars have speculated that he was slowly losing his mental powers due to Alzheimer's disease. Manuel Trevijano Etcheverria (1976, 168) supports an "embarrassment" reading and offers a possible motivation for such a feeling on Kant's part. Etcheverria refers to *Optimism* as a "work Kant hated because of its exacerbated Leibnizian tone and the acceptance of Leibniz's "best possible world." Ernst Cassirer (1918, 59), on the other hand, dismisses the work as "no more than a hastily composed, academic occasional piece" but he points us to another clue in a footnote. This is that in a letter to Johann Gotthelf Lindner dated October 28, 1759 (cf. 10:19) Kant explains that his motivation for the work was to defend optimism against Crusius. Martin Schönfeld offers another possible motivation for Kant's embarrassment which is consistent with subsequent developments rather than just expressing a later dislike for *Optimism*.

Only five years after its composition, Kant would reject the *Optimism* essay and his own earlier defense of the Leibnizian concept of evil as the mere absence of good. (The claimed proportionality of reality, relative perfection, and goodness had implied evil is nothing.) (2000, 188)

The later work to which Schönfeld is referring here is *Negative Magnitudes* which is indeed ground-breaking with respect to his taxonomy of evil and which will be considered in the following chapter.

In sum, the gap between Kant's views in the Reflections and those in *Optimism* has not been successfully bridged, but again, if the characterization of Kant's pre-Critical period thought on theodicy as one of exploration is accepted, then failure to close the gap is not decisive. We will see later how Kant resolved these divergent early views.

NOTES

1. In the event Kant did not enter the competition which suggests that even his early thoughts on optimism/theodicy were still in a formative stage.
2. Hereafter *Optimism*.
3. In the early to mid-eighteenth-century, "optimism" and "theodicy" were largely synonymous, although, strictly speaking, a theodicy is just one example of optimistic philosophy. In this study the two words will be used as synonyms without, I trust, any distortion in exposition or analysis.
4. Leibniz refers to such proof in *Theodicy* §44.
5. References in this form are to *Theodicy* section number/page number from the Huggard translation.
6. The imbalance is also considered in *Failure* as the third type of counter-purposiveness, which theodicy seeks to explain.
7. References in this form are to the Epistle/Section of Pope's *Essay*.
8. A first-century BCE Roman revolutionary and traitor against whom many accusations of evil were laid.
9. Hereafter *Only Possible Argument*.
10. Author's translation.
11. For example, see §199/H251.
12. Michael Tooley (2012) defines this "as a purely deductive argument that attempts to show that there are certain facts about the evil in the world that are logically incompatible with the existence of God. One especially ambitious form of this . . . argument attempts to establish the very strong claim that it is logically impossible for it to be the case both that there is any evil at all, and that God exists."

Chapter 2

The Origin and Nature of Evil

If theodicy consists in a reasoned explanation for the co-existence of evil and a God with the conventional moral and "omni-" properties, then without a clear understanding of the types of evil being addressed and equally, those not being addressed, any examination of would-be theodicies would not be productive. Accordingly, evil as Kant viewed it will be discussed twice in this study, once now, and then in Part III, dealing with his late-Critical period.

At first sight the title of this chapter suggests a plan of work. First, investigate where evil comes from and then second, set out what types of evil there are and their various attributes. However, such a neat logical division is difficult to maintain in practice, as even Kant found, because, in describing how a particular evil arose, one unavoidably gives a partial account of its nature. However, even if the two aspects are inextricably interwoven in such a manner it is still important to account for each and this is the aim of the chapter.

In the previous chapter it was shown that the context in which Kant began to consider theodicy was thoroughly Leibnizian. In view of that, a good starting point is a restatement of Leibniz's taxonomy of evil:

> Evil may be taken metaphysically, physically and morally. *Metaphysical evil* consists in mere imperfection, *physical evil* in suffering and *moral evil* in sin. Now although physical evil and moral evil are not necessary, it is enough that by virtue of the eternal verities they may be possible. (§21/H136)

It can be noted immediately that whilst physical and moral evil are not necessary, metaphysical evil is excluded from Leibniz's rider and thus, by implication, necessary. This is consistent with the then-prevailing view that evil was a result of Creation's finitude. The act of creation involved God choosing to instantiate one world from amongst all those he contemplated. When one possible world is actualized, limitation inevitably results as some things which would have been possible in different worlds are now impossible in the instantiated one. To that extent, any created world is limited. Further, God is perfect goodness but what is created cannot equal God and so must contain less good. Hence it is imperfect in the sense meant by Leibniz (cf. §30/H141). These ideas are combined in identifying limitation as a shortfall in the good and, to the extent that it was less good, it was evil. Further, as this evil was *unavoidably* present in Creation, it was regarded as metaphysical. An example drawn from the physical world may help to illustrate this notion of shortfall. Heat is a phenomenon of molecular movement; the hotter an object the more the movement. When we say something is cold, in colloquial terms, we think of <cold> as something, it is in fact nothing, being merely a way of saying that the cold object has less molecular movement than a hot object. In the same way as <cold> is a shortfall in, or a lack of, molecular movement, a shortfall in goodness does not have a positive ontological status.

Leibniz's taxonomy names two further kinds of evil but, when it is asked what they consist in, his definition above can appear deceptively simple but non-trivial issues soon arise. When God created, the laws of nature in what had been up to that point only a possible world became fixed and actual. This meant that they would operate in an identical manner under identical physical conditions. Should they, due to the unavoidability of deviation be grouped under metaphysical evil in the Leibnizian taxonomy and described as natural evil as advanced by Maria Rosa Antognazza? (2014, 122ff.). Or should the sometimes-injurious consequences for humans of the laws of nature be included in Leibnizian physical evil as argued by Busche? (2013, 249). Second, how should the physical suffering which is often the result of moral evil be classified? Should it be included in physical evil or seen as an unavoidable consequence of moral evil and thus inseparable from it? Leibniz offers a partial answer when he includes in his category of suffering or physical evil that "one may say of physical evil, that God wills it often as a penalty owing to guilt" (§23/H137).

Fortunately, these uncertainties do not have to be resolved in this study with respect to Leibniz's taxonomy of evil, but they certainly have to be addressed in any taxonomy of evil advanced on Kant's behalf. It should be noted, at once, that Kant did not set out an explicit taxonomy of his own. Therefore, when his taxonomy is referred to, it is an implied one which I maintain can still be fairly derived from the pre-Critical works under consideration.

THE LAWS OF NATURE AND THEIR WORKINGS

Whilst Kant did not explicitly endorse the Leibnizian taxonomy, his understanding of this provided the datum against which he set out his first thoughts on evil. Kant considered two fundamental questions arising from the Leibnizian taxonomy. First, was the undoubted suffering caused to humans arising from nature's workings divine punishment for moral evil? Second, was it any form of evil at all? The major sources which will be mined to establish his position on these two key questions are *Universal Natural History and theory of the Heavens or Essay on the Constitution and Mechanical Origin of the Whole Universe according to Newtonian Principles*[1] of 1755, the three essays of 1756 written in response to the Lisbon Earthquake, and the later pre-Critical work *Only Possible Argument* of 1763. This latter work, despite its title, contains much valuable material on the laws of nature and any possible departure from these by way of miracles.

That said, a brief reference to some earlier material is also helpful. Kant's earliest statement on the laws of nature came as early as 1747 when he wrote in *Living Forces*[2] that "Leibniz believed that it was not proper for God's power and wisdom that He should be necessitated to continually renew the motion which He had communicated to His creation"[3] (*LF*, 1:58; author's translation). This passage not only shows that Kant appreciated that Leibniz held that the laws of nature were continual in operation but also that he understood the Leibnizian position on how Creation is maintained, itself an important matter to be taken up in detail later. Further, in the 1753/1754 Reflections 3703–5, Kant made a comparison between Pope's and Leibniz's systems of optimism in which he agreed with both men on the uninterrupted operation of universal laws of nature. First, Pope held that "plagues or earthquakes break not Heaven's design" which clearly grants primacy to the uninterrupted workings of unchanged laws of nature over any contingent harmful effects on human beings. Kant, moreover, saw that these laws "are not placed in relation to each other by any forced union into a harmonious scheme [but] will adapt themselves as if spontaneously to the attainment of purposes which are perfect" (*Refl*, 17:234). By "forced union," I take Kant to mean some divine direct intervention. Rather, he is claiming that the result of this adaptation is still perfection which is consistent with Pope's "whatever is, is right." Second, Kant's agreement with Leibniz can be seen when the latter asks "shall God, whose laws concern a good so universal that all of the world that is visible to us perchance enters into it as no more than a trifling accessory, be bound to depart from his laws, because they today displease the one and tomorrow the other?" (§205/H255). So, an intermediate conclusion is that Kant in his stance on the laws of nature was not so much charting a new direction but rather building on the stance shared by these two predecessors.

Of the major sources, *Universal Natural History* is the one where Kant establishes the required theoretical foundation for his eventual position.[4] The full title—*Universal Natural History and theory of the Heavens or Essay on the Constitution and Mechanical Origin of the Whole Universe according to Newtonian Principles*—does not fully reveal Kant's overall aim for the work. In addition to the endorsement of Newtonian principles, there is a second major objective to be secured. This is that adopting these Newtonian principles must nonetheless still result in a place for God in Kant's overall description of the physical world. Kant will not accept a God reduced to just an originator and architect. This interpretation of *Universal Natural History's* aim is shared by Schönfeld who sees this work as characterized by Kant's effort to reconcile physics with a divinely inspired purpose holding that Kant "[u]nwilling to accept a deterministic world-machine without provisions . . . had to articulate new accounts of purpose, freedom, and God that would supplement and qualify the Newtonian model of nature" (2000, 96). One does not have to look far for confirmation. In the Preface to *Universal Natural History*, Kant makes it clear that the work must not be set in a purely materialistic context but rather in one set by God's act of creation:

> If the universal laws of causation of matter are also a result of the highest plan, then they can presumably have no purpose other than that which strives to fulfil of their own accord that plan which the highest wisdom has set itself. (*UNH*, 1:223)

Another noteworthy aspect of the work is that all three parts have an epigraph drawn from Pope's *Essay on Man*. In examining Reflections 3703–5 we have already seen the importance of this work to Kant and its later citation shows that the impression which it made on him was not a passing one. The example heading Part One reinforces the above remarks regarding the work's aim with respect to God:

Is the great chain that draws all to agree
And drawn supports, upheld by God or thee? (*UNH*, 1:241)

In other words, the system of universal laws which Kant calls upon is maintained by God. We shall see, however, that Kant did not support the idea that God's maintenance was by continuous action or *ad hoc* interventions. This identity of views with Pope is reinforced again near the end of Kant's work when he includes the following with its reference to the *Kette der Natur*—the chain of nature, the *nexus rerum*:

What a chain, which from God its beginning takes, what natures,
From heavenly and earthly [natures], from angels [and] humans down to animals
From seraphim to the worm! O distance that eye can never,
Attain and contemplate,
From the infinite to you, from you to nought! (*UNH*, 1:365)

In this endorsement by Kant, man's non-centrality in Creation, an important component of his stance on nature's workings, is yet again emphasized. Man could only justly complain about these workings if he was Creation's centerpiece in the physical sense but this is not the case. Kant again considers the chain of nature in the second part of the late-Critical *Critique of the Power of Judgment,* Critique of the Teleological Power of Judgment, where he deals with man as Creation's telic centerpiece but in a moral sense rather than a physical one. Intriguingly, Kant recommends his readers to start at chapter 8 of *Universal Natural History.* It might seem an odd place to start were it not for the fact that the theologically and theodically important material is to be found there. In my view, that Kant directed his readers there offers further support to the claim that he strove to set the laws of nature in a divine context. The foregoing considerations all point toward the essential role that Kant saw as still reserved for God and chapter 8's opening provides an unequivocal statement of this:

> One cannot look at the universe without recognizing the most excellent order in its arrangement and the sure characteristics of the hand of God in the perfection of its relations. Reason, having considered and admired so much beauty, so much excellence, is rightly incensed at the bold foolishness that has the audacity to attribute all this to coincidence and fortuitous chance. The highest wisdom must have made the design and an infinite power carried it out, otherwise it would be impossible that so many intentions that come together for one purpose could be encountered in the constitution of the universe. (*UNH*, 1:331)

From the above, the key elements of Kant's position can be readily discerned. They are: (i) the observed order in the world comes from God (the highest wisdom);[5] (ii) this order is not a happenstance; and (iii) the most significant aspect of the observed order lies not in the order displayed by various individual phenomena but in their *systematic unity.* Kant had already highlighted this aspect in Reflection 3704 and he does so again later in *Only Possible Argument* (1763) where he writes:

> Everything which is produced by nature, in so far as it tends towards harmoniousness, order and usefulness, agrees, it is true, with God's purposes. But it also displays the characteristic of having originated from universal laws. The effects of such universal laws extend far beyond any such individual case. (*OPA*, 2:143)

Kant has here identified three possibilities for the order in Creation: (i) blind chance; (ii) God continuously and directly intervenes *ad hoc* with the underlying purpose of ensuring order in the world; and (iii) God provides for the universal laws of nature which then act to supply the detail. He dismisses

(i) just as he did previously in *Optimism* (cf. *Opt*, 2:29) but questions whether it is (ii) or (iii) which applies. Kant thinks that philosophers in general have a prejudice against (iii) since it appears that it "would be disputing God's governance of the world" (*UNH*, 1:332), not only equating it with blind chance but also challenging God's omnipotence. Nevertheless, Kant is quite clear; it is (iii) and not (ii) which applies. Again, it must be emphasized that Kant is not arguing from the ordered design to be found in individual creatures but for the coherence of the total system of nature. He holds that the laws of nature do not each have an individual necessity "but rather that they must have their origin in a single understanding as the ground and source of all beings" (*UNH*, 1:333).

The lasting scientific contribution of *Universal Natural History* is Kant's demonstration, using only Newtonian principles and relatively sparse observational data, how an original cosmic nebula of dust could form itself into the physical world we know today and he clearly sets out his aim in this regard:

> [T]hen I hope to found a sure conviction on incontrovertible grounds: *that the world recognizes a mechanical development out of the universal laws of nature as the origin of its constitution.* (*UNH*, 1:334; emphasis in original)

He proceeds to show, using Newton's laws, how the planets in our solar system and galaxies were formed and even how apparent irregularities such as comets can be accounted for. However, this impressive scientific detail, reprised later by Laplace, does not directly concern us here and sadly must be passed over. What is relevant from the account is that Kant considered that he had shown that not only was there order in the world but also that that order did *not* result from God's *direct* action. Also important here, are certain elements of the Leibniz-Clarke correspondence. This covered many topics including God's nature and that of time and space, but the aspect central to this enquiry is this same issue, namely the nature of God's maintenance of the world. Leibniz positions the issue in his first paper (L1:4).[6]

> Sir Isaac Newton and his followers[7] have also a very odd opinion concerning the work of God. According to their doctrine, God Almighty wants to wind up his watch from time to time: otherwise it would cease to move.... [God] must consequently be so much the more unskillful a workman, as he is oftener obliged to mend his work and set it right.

In other words, in Leibniz's eyes, the Newtonians' claim undermined God's perfection and/or His omnipotence with their implication that He did not do the job properly in the first place. Clarke rejected this accusation with the following which has a hint of occasionalism:

[H]e [God] not only composes or puts things together, but is himself the author and continual preserver of their original forces and moving powers: and consequently 'tis not a diminution, but the true glory of his workmanship, that nothing is done without his *continual* government and inspection. (Emphasis added)

From these extracts, two distinct positions concerning God's possible role can be distinguished. In the first position, helpfully described as "divine operational presence" by Ezio Vailati (1997, 18), God intervenes in the world—the "hands-on" chief executive as it were. This is the Newtonian position. The second position, again borrowing from Vailati is described by him as "divine situational presence." This is where God is the world's conserver, the chairman of the board, removed from "day-to-day" management but retaining a benevolent supervisory watch on His Creation—a sort of "soft" deism. This is the Leibnizian position. However, whilst this differentiation is interesting, what is paramount here is the position adopted by Kant.

Kant holds that at a certain point Newton gave up on explanation and referred to God's direct will (cf. *UNH*, 1:339). Kant does not and considers that that laws of nature as described by Newton are sufficient to explain all the workings of the heavens. In this way Kant is a Leibnizian in this matter. Indeed, as L. W. Beck pithily puts it, Kant "out-Newtoned" Newton (1969, 431). Or in Loades's fuller version, "by employing Newtonian physics Kant could eliminate appeal to the intervention of the deity where even the Newtonians had supposed it to be necessary" (1985, 102).

From these considerations, two significant provisional conclusions applicable to theodicy can be drawn. First, in arguing that the laws of nature can fully describe the workings of the cosmos, Kant has implicitly rejected the notion of God's *direct* actions causing physical harm. By implication too, he has at least downplayed miracles which would be *ad hoc* rather than constant interventions but still interference by God in the workings of the laws of nature which He has put in place. Second, Kant's considerations confirm that for him there is a God but He is no longer the ongoing maintainer of the universe's detailed workings in the sense of continuous intervention. God is still recognized, nonetheless, as the creator of the pre-universal nebula upon which the laws of nature operated as Newton set out and Kant used in his account of how the universe was formed. This point is theodically significant because if God was eliminated from Kant's system by a purely naturalistic/materialistic account of the universe, then the need for a theodicy would also be eliminated. Moreover, God is not only the source of these laws of nature and their unified action but is also their conserving cause in the sense that He underwrites them and guarantees their continuity.[8] It is this which prevents Kant being accused of deism, or at least a "hard" deism where God has nothing further to do with His Creation. This is important for this study since this would have placed quite different demands on any attempted theodicy. For Kant that God is a "situational" rather than an "operational" presence (in Vailati's terminology) does not matter in terms of divine action; it is just a timing issue as he sets out in *Only Possible Argument*:

> [F]or whether it takes place gradually, at different times, the degree of the supernatural is no greater in the second case than it is in the first. The only difference between them relates not to the degree of the immediate divine action but merely to the *when.* (*OPA*, 2:115)

Here Kant is seeing the workings of the laws of nature as a form of continual but indirect creation on God's part even though the result of their working is fixed. But he is unequivocal that when the laws of nature are recognized as ordering nature in detail, the importance of, and the dependence on, God is in no way diminished.

If *Universal Natural History* is where Kant established the theory, then it is the earthquake essays where he puts it into practice. In 1756 Kant wrote three essays in response to the 1755 Lisbon earthquake which not only shook Portugal physically but which also, intellectually, made European thought on God and evil rock on its foundations. At a considerable distance in time from this event and with a very different *Weltanschauung*, it is easy to underestimate the significance of the Lisbon earthquake, occurring as it did in the great capital of a world-wide Christian empire. But it was as profound a challenge to the moral philosophy of Kant's day as Auschwitz is to ours. In particular, it threatened to undermine optimism as it was expressed in Leibniz's *Theodicy*[9] and reinforce the views of those who saw such calamities as divine punishment. These three short essays were Kant's immediate response. The essays are largely given over to geophysical speculation about the causes of earthquakes which although scientifically intriguing does not concern us here. Again, Schönfeld provides a succinct summary with which to position the essays:

> The three papers [the earthquake essays] revealed that he [Kant] was more interested in the scientific side of the event, in the question how it happened, than in the metaphysical problem of why it happened. He had already asserted in the *Universal Natural History* that the cosmic evolution of nature towards self-perfection may involve local destructions. Hence, the Lisbon earthquake did not challenge his cosmogony in the same way as it did Leibniz's theodicy. (2000, 75)

The consideration here will be limited to just the second essay[10] as here are the passages which are most relevant to the metaphysical problem of *why* it happened. In them Kant ponders whether such natural disasters are evil. One such passage considers the laws of nature to be regular in their working and that all their unpleasant consequences are natural:

> Even the terrible instruments by which disaster is visited on mankind, the shattering of countries, the fury of the sea shaken to its foundations, the fire-spewing mountains,[11] invite man's contemplation, and are planted in nature by God as a proper consequence of fixed laws. (*EE2*, 1:431)

Another passage concerns our unwarranted assumptions about man's physical centrality in Creation, that the world should be arranged for our comfort, and the sense that we have somehow been falsely wronged:

> [T]hereby, it humbles humanity in that it allows it to see that it has no right . . . to expect from the laws of nature that God has ordered purely agreeable consequences, and it probably teaches also in this manner to see: that this playground of his desires should not contain the objective of all his [God's] intentions. (Ibid.)[12]

Two important points stand out here. First, we can see that Kant considers that man cannot expect to avoid deleterious consequences from the workings of nature's laws. Second, Kant states that man and this earth being "the playground of his desires" is not the sole objective in God's plan in Creation. Neither point is new; we have seen these already made, once in Reflections 3703–5 where Kant found that both Leibniz and Pope expressed themselves in a similar manner, and again in the earlier discussion of *Universal Natural History*.

Most significantly, in the *Schlußbetrachtung*[13] of this second essay Kant, for the first but not the only time, breaks any possible link between moral and physical evil when he maintains that the latter is not a punishment for the former, stating:

> One offends completely against this [our love for our fellow man in his misery], however, when one at any time regards such fate as imposed punishment that will hit the concerned cities for their evil deeds and when we view these misfortunes as the goal of the avenging God as his justice that flows over all. (*EE2*, 1:459)

The passage also suggests that not only do we wrong our neighbor when we accuse him of moral evil on the evidence of the physical evil he experiences, but we also offend against God's justice. Kant will strongly reinforce this point later in his treatment of Job's troubles in *Failure*. In addition to breaking the link between moral and physical evil, Kant goes further and sees that in addition to any attempt to make or maintain the link being wrong, it is presumptuous on man's part since it depends on a claimed insight into God's ways (cf. *EE2*, 1:459–60). This is another key issue for Kant on Job in *Failure* where he will dismiss all attempts at philosophical theodicy using the same principle.

When we look to *Only Possible Argument*, we find that Kant confirms the stance which he adopted in this second Earthquake Essay, namely that those events which could be termed natural evil are not evil at all but just the consequences of the laws of nature:

> Furthermore, the occurrence of these events [destructive forces] from time to time is sufficiently grounded in the constitution of nature, according to a universal law. But the vices and moral corruption of human race are not *natural* grounds connected with these events, nor are they to be numbered among the laws in accordance with which they take place.... And that attribution implies that the event in question was a misfortune, not a punishment: man's moral conduct cannot be a cause of earthquakes according to natural law, for there is no connection here between the cause and the effect. (*OPA*, 2:104)

Moreover, in this passage and explicitly for the first time, Kant is stating that there is nothing lawlike about moral evil. Moral infringement does not result from some form of natural moral law in the same non-contingent manner in which physical events flow from the laws of nature. In doing this he is decisively distancing himself from Pope's "whatever is, is right" including the evil of a Borgia with which he may have toyed earlier in Reflection 3704.

Although Kant's position on miracles, namely at least downplaying if not rejecting them outright, could be reasonably extrapolated from his views on the laws of nature in *Universal Natural History* and the earthquake essays, in *Only Possible Argument* he provides us with explicit evidence for this in which he differentiates between natural and supernatural events. He holds that there are two essential requirements for an event to be considered natural. An event which does not meet both requirements Kant holds to be supernatural and thus a miracle but he usefully distinguishes between two cases of the supernatural. First, those cases where the efficient cause is completely external to nature he terms "materially supernatural." Second, those cases where "the forces of nature are directed to producing the effect is not itself subject to a rule of nature" (*OPA*, 2:104), Kant terms "formally supernatural." In other words, in the first case God would be causing a miracle which was completely at odds with the laws of nature which He has put in place and in the second He would be intervening to direct the forces of nature to realize a desired end (cf. *OPA*, 2:105). The latter is closer to those who held that physical punishment was a divine response to moral evil as claimed by some after the Lisbon earthquake. They did not question that earthquakes or typhoons were natural events but these were somehow directed by God and targeted the morally guilty. Now if Kant were to accept that God acted in either a materially or formally supernatural manner, this would run counter to three firm views which are essential features of the position which he has established with respect to the laws of nature that God has put in place. These are (i) that God does not need to wind up Creation's clock (contra Newton but not Leibniz), (ii) that the laws of nature are universal and continuous in operation (in agreement with Leibniz and Pope), and (iii) that natural harm is not a divine punishment for moral evil (contra Leibniz). Whilst Kant did not and indeed could not explicitly argue for miracles' impossibility, to nevertheless allow a place for them in his system and thus rejecting the three standpoints above would require a *volte-face* totally out of character. To allow miracles but still to remain subscribed to these three views would be inconsistent. Neither accusation is leveled at Kant here especially as Kant provides an explicit statement of his position: "Where nature operates in accordance with necessary laws, there will be no need for God to correct the course of events by direct intervention" (*OPA*, 2:110).

Kant also links miracles' inadmissibility with the notion of a best possible world when he states that "indeed, I should find it amazing if anything occurred or could occur in the course of nature in accordance with general laws which was displeasing to God, or in need of a miracle to improve it" (*OPA*, 2:115). An interesting corollary to Kant's stance flows from this. Because Kant sees that God does not directly intervene in the world, it puts the onus on Him to select, at the outset, that world where the laws of nature yield the most perfect result possible. Anything less would be inconsistent with God's own perfection, a position taken by Kant. In consequence, his divine non-interventionism adds weight to Leibniz's case that this world is indeed the best possible, at least in the physical sense.

When the evidence from *Universal Natural History*, the second Earthquake Essay, and *Only Possible Argument* is weighed, two far-reaching moves can be seen which also act to remove, in Kant's case, some of the uncertainties discussed earlier with respect to Leibniz's taxonomy. First, the contingent deleterious effects on human beings flowing from the workings of the laws of nature in earthquakes, typhoons, and the like cannot be described as any form of evil. This is not to deny that suffering, often grievous, occurs in the wake of such natural disasters but evil it is not. In this way, it does not matter for Kant whether such events are a component of metaphysical evil resulting from the limitations inherent in Creation or are an element in what Leibniz terms physical evil. It is simply natural harm. Kant recognizes that evil and harm are different, although we must jump forward temporarily to Kant's late-Critical period and his *Critique of Practical Reason* (*CPR*,

5:59–60) to find explicit confirmation. In the second *Critique* Kant states that "[t]he German language has the good fortune to possess expressions which do not allow this difference to be overlooked." Specifically, whereas Latin has one word, *malum* (and English too—evil), German has two words, *Böse* and *Übel*, and Kant uses these words with precision (which will be seen to be of relevance later in *Failure*). *Böse* means "evil" and *Übel* "ill-being" or "woe," which is consistent with the term "harm" being used here. Although in the second *Critique* Kant is primarily concerned with moral issues, the differentiation which he makes there is directly applicable to our considerations here. This can be seen when Kant confirms that the term evil does not apply to a person's physical state when he gave the example of the Stoic who refused to acknowledge that pain from gout was any form of evil (cf. *CPR*, 5:60). Second, because Kant has discounted God interfering with the laws of nature through miracles, physical evil cannot be a divine punishment for moral delinquency. In modern terms, it is not God's corrective or retributive justice. This is contra Leibniz at (§23/H137) as noted above. Kant and Leibniz differed fundamentally on how possible divine punishment related to God's justice which both men nevertheless saw as an essential moral attribute of God. It was suggested earlier in the chapter that at *EE2*, 1:459 Kant saw divine punishment through physical suffering as offending against God's justice. In contrast, Leibniz, when confirming his stance on physical evil as punishment sees it as an unavoidable consequence of this same justice. He states:

> It is therefore not God who is the cause of moral evil: but he is the cause of physical evil, that is, the punishment of moral evil. And this punishment, far from being incompatible with the supremely good principle, of necessity emanates from that one of its attributes, I mean its justice, which is not less essential to it than its goodness. (§155/H220)

These two conclusions have a significant effect on any theodicy in a Kantian context. Now that the effects of the workings of the laws of nature which were previously described as either physical or natural evil are not evil at all, there is less evil which any would-be theodicy has to rationally reconcile with God's moral attributes. Further, now that physical evil does not signify divine punishment, there is no need to account for the miracles which would otherwise have been needed to deliver such an effect.

It is useful to take stock at this point and take a brief look back at Leibniz's taxonomy of evil to see what remains to be accounted for in a theodicy which could be put forward on Kant's behalf. When this is done there are three aspects which Kant has not (yet) addressed: (i) evil as limitation; (ii) the suffering that results from moral evil; and (iii) moral evil itself. That Kant addresses (i) and (iii) will be seen in the consideration of *Attempt to Introduce the Concept of Negative Magnitudes in Philosophy* (1763),[14] which follows.

NEGATIVE MAGNITUDES AND THE NATURE OF EVIL

Negative Magnitudes is the second major work with direct relevance to any taxonomy of evil ascribed to Kant. Given the pivotal importance which I judge the work to have in the development of Kant's thought on evil, a brief review of its standing in the literature is worthwhile. It is surprisingly little considered. Here I am agreeing with Melissa Zinkin who states in her paper "Kant on Negative Magnitudes" that the work "is one of the least frequently discussed of all his [Kant's] pre-critical writings" (2012, 397).[15] However, Zinkin's paper, after a short exposition of Kant's early views on negative magnitudes, concentrates on the metaphysical aspects of the work as she is principally concerned to show how some of Kant's metaphysical views in *Negative Magnitudes* were carried forward into his Critical philosophy. Similar approaches, investigating only the metaphysical implications, were taken both by Christian Kanzian in his 1993 paper "Kant und Crusius" and Robert Schnepf in his 2001 paper "Metaphysik oder Metaphysikritik." To date, I have found little consideration of the work's moral philosophical impact, including in Andrew Chignell's 2009 and 2012 papers, which touch on *Negative Magnitudes*.

However, if *Negative Magnitudes* suffers from a lack of consideration in modern scholarship then, in the past, it clearly made an impact on at least one famous philosopher. Eva Engel draws attention to this in her paper "Mendelssohn contra Kant" in which she highlights the work's significance for the former. She states, that "[i]n April 1764 Mendelssohn had, at the end of his discussion of space-time, put Kant's term [negative magnitudes] under the public spotlight and indicated the wish that this spectacular development continued" (2004, 270).[16] Engel also calls on Mendelssohn himself in support of her stance:

> The difference, that he [Kant] makes ... in the intention of the *compossibilitatis realitatum* in God between the logical and the real repugnance, seems grounded, and worthy of closer examination by the philosophical reader and an application to be recommended.

Taking our lead from Mendelssohn, a closer examination does indeed yield much of value. By applying the underlying principle of *Negative Magnitudes*, Kant's stance on evil underwent far-reaching change to one where two types of evil were admitted. Whilst Kant continued to see some evil as arising from limitation, there was also now a type of evil which was ontologically real. In the Preface to *Negative Magnitudes* Kant explains that it is his intention to "consider a concept which is familiar enough in mathematics but which is still very unfamiliar in philosophy; and I wish to consider this concept in relation to philosophy itself" (*NM*, 2:169) before setting out the underlying principle on which his thesis was based:

> For negative magnitudes are not negations of magnitudes, as the similarity of the expressions has suggested, but something truly positive in itself, albeit something opposed to the positive magnitude. And thus negative attraction is not rest, as *Crusius* supposed, but genuine repulsion. (*NM*, 2:169)

Kant then identifies two types of opposition between which, in his view, philosophers to date had not differentiated. First, there is logical opposition upon which "attention has been exclusively and uniquely concentrated until now" (*NM*, 2:171).[17] Logical opposition "consists in the fact that something is simultaneously affirmed and denied of the very same thing. The consequence of the logical conjunction is *nothing at all* (*nihil negativum irrepresentabile*)." Second, there is real opposition which is "two predicates of a thing are opposed to each other, but not through the law of contradiction. Here one thing is cancelled by another, but the consequence is *something*" (ibid.). In this way Kant is presenting us with two quite different concepts. The first is the nothing of incoherence, is it literally "no thing," whilst the second is equilibrium from cancelling equal and opposites but still a *something*.

He then assigns an algebraic values and names to logical opposition calling the result of logical opposition "nothing: zero = 0; its meaning is negation, lack, absence" (*NM*, 2:172). With respect to real opposition he states that "no magnitude can be called absolutely negative: "+a" and "–a" must each be called the negative magnitude of the other" (*NM*, 2:174). In other words, Kant is asserting that ontologically negative things don't exist. Opposites are real and are only prefixed with a plus sign or a minus sign by mathematical convention. Putting these two notions together, an example would be that a lack of pleasure (0) is not the opposite of pleasure (p); that is displeasure (–p), or in Kant's words, "displeasure is accordingly not simply a lack, [but] a positive sensation . . . which, wholly or partly, cancels the pleasure which arises from another ground" (*NM*, 2:182). These considerations allow Kant to set out two fundamental rules[s], the first being: "a real repugnancy only occurs where there are two things, as *positive grounds,* and where one of them cancels the consequence of the other" (*NM*, 2:175). However, he adds the caveat that "determinations which conflict with each other must exist in the same subject." It is helpful to take up Kant's example of a ship sailing westward from Portugal to Brazil against an east-going current. If west-going movement is denoted by "+" and east-going by "−," then in his example the net movement for the week is by +12+7−3−5+8 = 19 miles. The ship's movement through the water westwards was 27 miles but this was reduced by the water moving eastwards 8 miles. The movement west and east have been denoted plus and minus respectively but there is nothing inherently positive about moving west or negative about moving east. Both movements are ontologically real with a positive ground. Again, we are only assigning a plus or a minus sign to them by mathematical convention. However, the wind and the current do not oppose each other[18]; they only do so through a third thing, the ship "the same subject."

Expanding Kant's example a little brings out the point which he is keen to emphasize. Suppose that ship's movements were now +12+7+8−13−5−9 miles. The net movement would now be zero. Kant terms this *equilibrium* but it is still a *something* in Kant's view. This situation contrasts with that where neither wind nor current are acting upon it and the ship is at *rest*. The net effect is the same but the explanation for the lack of movement with respect to the seabed is quite different. Later Kant applies this consideration to moral actions/inactions and when he does so it is theodically important.

The second fundamental rule which Kant sets out in this matter "is really the reverse of the first . . . whenever there is a positive ground and the consequence is nonetheless zero then there is real opposition. In other words: this ground is connected with another positive ground" (*NM*, 2:177). This implies also that in a state of equilibrium if only one ground is known, it is incumbent on us to search for the second. An example from the physical world illustrates this. If we only knew about gravitational attraction, we would be searching for another force to explain why the earth is in a stable heliocentric orbit.[19] However, the most significant statement of the first part of the treatise is made almost at its end where Kant gives his definition of terms which feature prominently in his predecessors' taxonomies of evil.[20]

> A negation, in so far as it is the consequence of a real opposition [*Realrepugnanz*], will be designated *deprivation (privatio)*.[21] But any negation, in so far as it does not arise from this type of repugnancy will be called a *lack (defectus, absentia)*.[22] (Ibid.)

Thus, a negation coming from a real opposition is termed a privatio. This is the term which had been used by Kant's predecessors to indicate that some attribute is missing from an entity the concept of which normally contains the missing attribute. To my mind, Kant is using the term in the same way. This is indicated by his using the German word "Beraubung," here translated as "deprivation." This is helpful as the word is derived from "*rauben*"—"to rob." The entity has been "robbed" of something that is proper to it. An example would be a human being without legs since the concept <human being> contains the possession of legs. In other words, it describes something which is incorrectly absent, namely, a part which should be found in a realized entity corresponding to the concept but which is missing. It is worth emphasizing here that Kant is quite clear here that, when he is talking about a real opposition, there must be two positive grounds in opposition. The two grounds are the possession of legs which can be assigned a positive value and the removal of legs as a result of amputation can be assigned a negative value. The result is no legs but the privation is still *something* on Kant's terms. We will see later that, when he applies *Realrepugnanz* to the moral matters which concern us, there is also an opposition.

With the other form of negation, which for Kant can only be a logical opposition, he is less helpful calling it amongst other things a lack or a defect. In everyday language this can also suggest that some attribute is missing from an entity that is proper to its concept. Here the German word which Kant uses *"Mangel"* does not help either since this denotes a lack, defect or fault. The last word which Kant uses is *absentia*—an absence and this is more fitting as it agrees better with his designation of a logical opposition as *nothing at all* or zero: = 0 or, more generally, what is correctly absent. An example would be a fish without legs, the latter being no part of the concept <fish>. It has not been robbed of legs. However, there is still scope for terminological confusion as the absence of an attribute not part of the concept of an entity is called a *negatio* by others yet Kant has used "negation" to describe both forms of opposition. To avoid equivocation, it is my intention where possible to use Kant's third word, *absentia*.[23]

Having laid the terminological foundation, Kant makes the far-reaching move alluded to earlier:

> The error into which many philosophers[24] have fallen [is] . . . that they generally treat evils as if they were mere negations,[25] even though it is obvious from our explanations that there are evils of lack (*mala defectus*) [*absentia*] and evils of deprivation (*mala privationis*). Evils of lack are negations [*absentia*]: there is no ground for the positing of what is opposed to them. Evils of deprivation presuppose that there are positive grounds which cancel the good for which there really exists another ground. Such evils of deprivation are *negative* goods. (*NM*, 2:182)

A fundamental change has occurred. In contrast to regarding evil purely as a lack of good, there is now incontrovertible evidence that Kant now recognizes an additional and distinct type of evil. Moreover, he makes two further points which merit attention. First, that *mala defectus* (*absentia*) can nevertheless still be evil. Second, the way opens for Kant to differentiate between the traditional religious terms "sins of omission" (*absentia*) and "sins of commission" (*privatio*). Kant supports this differentiation with the example of not giving to a person in need whom one has a moral duty to help (*absentia*) in contrast to robbing that person (*privatio*). They are both evils differing only in degree. In other words, man is driven by inner moral feeling and thus conscious of his inner moral duty and so a sin of omission is not zero in Kant's view but still a negative only differing in magnitude from a sin of commission (cf. *NM*, 2:183).

Thus, Kant seems now to be saying that an absentia, a lack, is not really zero on the scale of evil as he does at *NM*, 2:172 but a lesser negative. To resolve this difficulty, it is helpful to jump forward to his definitive *Religion* (cf. *Rel*, 6:22n) where Kant restates his argument from *Negative Magnitudes* in unequivocal terms. He makes it clear that the zero of inaction results not from no forces acting but the good and bad working against each other as in the case of not helping the person in need. In the case of sins of commission, the evil outweighs the good rather than just cancelling it out and a morally bad action ensues. In the case of sins of omission, the evil cancels out the good and results in the morally questionable inaction of equilibrium. However, I maintain that this nuance does not undermine the principal outcome of Kant's considerations, namely that there are now two types of evil, moral evil and metaphysical evil conceived as limitation.

With this conclusion I am agreeing with Heinz Heimsoeth who states in his paper, "*Zum Kosmotheologischen Ursprung der Kantischen Freiheitsantinomie,*"[26] that:

> In *Negative Magnitudes* Kant first introduced the idea of the "Realrepugnanz" and, from the mathematical and natural sciences, also has extended it to the psychological (with later expression: on the data of the "inner sense"). And then the principle here is also still applied to the contrast of good and evil—contrary to all views that "iniquity" might be mere privation.[27] (1966, 227)

In other words, for Kant, our considerations to do good or evil are governed, just like the ship on its way to Brazil, by resolving two opposing "forces." In my view, there is no doubt that that this is Kant's substantive position since, as noted, he sets out this same argument of opposition explicitly applied to good and evil once more in the late-Critical *Religion* of 1791 (cf. *Rel*, 6:22n). Also, in that later work, Kant introduces the notions of a "propensity to evil" and a "pre-disposition to the good" and whilst Kant's treatment of these notions goes considerably deeper, fundamentally, they are two opposing "forces." Just as in the case of the earth's orbit mentioned earlier, when we know that we should do the good thing and yet do nothing, there must be another "force" restraining us, the bad thing. Further support for the concept of *Realrepugnanz* applied to morality can be drawn from *Failure* where Kant opposes God's holiness as law-giver with moral evil, God's goodness opposes the physically counter-purposive, and God's justice opposes the disproportion in the world between evil and punishment. A possible objection is that this breaks Kant's stricture that the opposition must occur in the same third object and that here divine properties are being compared incorrectly with human or natural ones. A counter would be that they do indeed occur in a common third object, the world. That support comes from *Religion* and *Failure* is noteworthy since these are late-Critical works. This shows that despite my characterization of Kant's pre-Critical period as generally one of exploration, here I contend, there is lasting, career-long, change.

So, with *Negative Magnitudes*, Kant's notion of evil underwent a far-reaching change, moving to something which was not only inherent in human beings due to their createdness but additionally something real to be done or not done. This conclusion is shared by Schönfeld. We have already seen in chapter 1 that he offered another possible motivation for Kant's embarrassment about *Optimism* (2000, 188) but one which was consistent with subsequent developments rather than merely expressing a later dislike. The subsequent development to which Schönfeld is referring is *Negative Magnitudes*. The implications for any attempted theodicy are fundamental. When evil was seen solely as a limitation of Creation it was possible to argue that evil was not of man's choosing but inherent in the created world and thus God was responsible for the introduction of evil through the act of creation. Now that evil can also be something ontologically real the way is clear for Kant to develop an account of human responsibility for evil through freedom. This could yet mean some responsibility on God's part but now of a very different nature.

Having now considered the available textual resources, it is a suitable point at which to take stock. The issues which had not been dealt with prior to considering *Negative Magnitudes* were (i) evil as limitation; (ii) the suffering that results from much moral evil; and (iii) moral evil itself. Concerning (i), at *NM*, 2:182, Kant recognizes its existence and accordingly it is fair to still include it in any taxonomy of evil which could be ascribed to him. With respect to (ii), he is silent and thus we have no guide whether to retain physical evil as a category now only containing the suffering which results from moral evil. The alternative would be to regard such suffering as integral to moral evil with both the evil act and the consequent suffering placed under the term "moral evil." To prevent this uncertainty being raised each time moral evil is discussed, I will adopt the latter case, namely as part of the moral evil. An example would be the pain experienced by the victim of torture being grouped together with the moral evil committed by the torturer. With respect to (iii), Kant has not used the term "moral evil,"[28] but I hold that it can be used fairly on his behalf as a category since there are examples where he gives every indication of agreement with Leibniz. Supporting this, the latter regards moral evil as sin and that in *Negative Magnitudes,* when discussing evil, Kant refers to sins both of commission and omission. Elsewhere, he refers to the "vices and moral corruption of human race" (*OPA*, 2:104). At *NM*, 2:182 there are references to "evil of lack" and "evil of deprivation," and in the second Earthquake essay Kant refers to "evil deeds." So, I regard gathering all these descriptions under the term "moral evil" is a reasonable step.

I am now in a position to put forward a taxonomy of evil on Kant's behalf for further use in this study—again an implied taxonomy. There are two categories remaining after discounting physical evil and natural evil.

- Metaphysical Evil—conceived as limitation
- Moral Evil—the evil done and the consequent suffering

The challenge for any would-be theodicy at this stage of the study is twofold. First, evil as limitation must be addressed. Here two alternatives would seem to be open for a theodicy's promoter. Either (i) an account is required that removes God's *prima facie* responsibility for production of a world where evil was unavoidably present through the createdness of the world, or (ii) evil as limitation must be eliminated from the taxonomy of evil against which the theodicy is set. Second, moral evil as evil done is seemingly the direct responsibility of human beings. If so, the role of an omniscient God in bringing about these beings as part of Creation, and in this way seeming to bear an indirect responsibility for evil must be addressed in any successful theodicy. This is an issue that Kant must ultimately address. In the following chapter this topic will be discussed further.

NOTES

1. Hereafter *Universal Natural History.*
2. Full title *Thoughts on the True Estimation of Living Forces.*
3. Interestingly, this citation continues "as Mr. Newton imagined," which suggests that Kant understood one of the bones of contention between Leibniz and Clarke. The latter, a Newtonian, held to the idea of immediate sustainment by God of gravitational force. This is also remarked upon by Kant at 1:415 in *New Elucidation.* For a fuller account see Antognazza (2009, 534–38).
4. Kant's Newtonian conversion could be held to date from 1754 and the "spin cycle" essay where he acknowledged the explanatory power of Newton's laws.
5. This is an interesting reversal of the physico-theological proof of God's existence which argues from order to God. The simultaneous adoption of both arguments

was one of the two serious problems signalled by Kant in Reflection 3705 and which were considered in chapter 1.

6. References given in this form are to Leibniz paper: section, as presented in Alexander (1956).

7. Including Samuel Clarke, Newton's representative and defender in the correspondence.

8. Kant reiterates this point at *OPA*, 2:115.

9. Again this relied on misunderstanding Leibniz's theodicy as an *a posteriori* argument from the alleged evil of the earthquake, not on an *a priori* one which tried to account for evil *in general* in the world.

10. History and Natural Description of the Most Exceptional Occurrences of the Earthquakes, which shook a large part of the Earth at the end of 1755.

11. Lisbon had indeed suffered earthquake, tsunami, and fire on All Saints Day 1755.

12. Except where stated otherwise, all translations in the treatment of the earthquake essays are mine.

13. Final consideration.

14. Hereafter *Negative Magnitudes*.

15. A search of both *Kant-Studien* and *Kantian Review* yields only one paper with "Negative Magnitudes" in its title, that of Zinkin.

16. All translations from German, with the exception of those from primary texts, are mine except where stated otherwise.

17. Zinkin (2012, 397) concurs seeing it as "a criticism of rationalist logic, which only includes logical opposition."

18. Except for minor "wind over tide" frictional surface effects.

19. Of course, this second force *is* known to us as centrifugal force.

20. A full and instructive history of the terminology in the taxonomies of evil is given in Antognazza (2014, 115ff.).

21. *Beraubung*.

22. *Mangel*.

23. Except when citing Kant, the original will be retained with *absentia* added in square parentheses.

24. It is unhelpful that Kant does not specify who these philosophers are that he has in mind. Antognazza (2014, 115ff.) has shown that the position of Kant's predecessors is much more nuanced and that the use of identical terms by them is far from unequivocal.

25. Kant reinforces this point when he states "Vice (*demeritum*) is not merely a negation; it is a negative virtue (*meritum negativum*)" (*NM*, 2:182).

26. On the cosmo-theological origin of the Kantian antinomy of freedom.

27. Heimsoeth's use of the word "privation" does not agree with that set out by Kant. Here it is being used in the sense of *absentia*. This illustrates the lack of standardised definitions in the literature for key terms used when describing evil which can easily derail debate on this topic.

28. Kant will do so in the late-Critical *Failure*.

Chapter 3

Is Philosophical Theodicy Possible for Kant?

I contend that in his pre-Critical period, in contrast to his late-Critical period, Kant held that philosophical theodicies were possible. The aim of the chapter is to substantiate this. However, some further preliminary work must first be done. There are three essential components in a would-be theodicy: evil, God, and human freedom. The first component, evil, was investigated in the previous chapter with the outcome that moral evil is one of the two elements of the implicit taxonomy of evil put forward on Kant's behalf. The other two components, God and human freedom, must now be addressed. For evil to be classified as moral in the first place implies that persons must bear responsibility for the evil done or suffered. To be responsible requires that they could have done otherwise. That is to say, they made a free choice for the evil concerned. So the first question to be answered is whether Kant, at this stage of his career, has established an account of human freedom sufficiently robust for this purpose. The second question is perhaps so obvious that it can be easily overlooked. Namely, in the pre-Critical period, on what foundation does Kant's position rest that there *is* a God whose moral attributes require rational reconciliation with evil? As stated previously, theodicy requires a *Theos*.

DOES THE PRE-CRITICAL KANT HAVE AN ACCOUNT OF FREEDOM?

In order to answer this question it essential to examine the *New Elucidation of the First Principles of Metaphysical Cognition*[1] of 1755 as this is the principal pre-Critical work in which Kant considers freedom. The particular focus is on Proposition IX (*NE*, 1:398–406), which deals with what he terms the "determining ground." Kant is fully cognizant of the threat posed by necessitation since if we are fully necessitated in all our actions, moral and physical, any defense of God's holiness, benevolence, and justice in the face of moral evil cannot get off the ground. Kant certainly sees Crusius as the main opponent to be defeated if he, Kant, is to give an account of freedom which is sufficient for the ascription of moral responsibility to humans. Kant fully understands the implications of a failure to do so and the Crusian argument succeeding with its confirmation that "all things happen in virtue of a natural conjunction, and in such a connected and continuous fashion that, if someone were to wish the opposite of some event or even of a free action, his wish would involve the conception of something impossible" (*NE*, 1:399). However, he immediately seeks to demolish the argument from Crusius:

> [I]n the case of the free actions of human beings: in so far as they are regarded as determinate, their opposites are excluded; they are not, however, excluded by grounds which are posited as existing outside the desires and spontaneous inclinations of the subject as if the agent were compelled to perform his actions against his will . . . and as a result of a certain ineluctable necessity. (*NE*, 1:400)

Here, Kant is clearly not only asserting than human beings are free in their decisions and thus can act to initiate causal chains but is also discriminating between actions having a determining ground and being necessitated. All actions have a determining ground even when arising from the use of human freedom to choose. Moreover, once an action is taken, an alternative action is clearly not concurrently possible. However, the opposite is not excluded as impossible prior to the freedom to chose being exercised as would be the case with necessitation.

Kant's primary method of teasing out the various issues surrounding the threat of necessitation is to offer a dialogue between two imaginary characters, Caius and Titius. The dialogue opens with Caius looking back on his misdeeds and expressing the hope that what he supposes is Titius's stance is correct and that he, Caius, is not responsible for his misdeeds after all:

> *Caius*: But on your [Titius's] view, every inclination of my will has been completely determined by an antecedent ground and that, in turn, by another antecedent ground, and so on right back to the beginning of things. (*NE*, 1:402)

But Titius at once destroys Caius's hope by reminding him that:

> [*Titius*]: At any given juncture, the series of interconnected grounds furnishes motives for the performance of the action which are equally attractive in both directions: you readily adopted one of them because acting thus rather than otherwise was more pleasurable to you. (*NE*, 1:402)

In other words, everything up to the moment of Caius's choice, including the available choices themselves had, and must have had in order for the choice to exist, determining grounds but it was Caius who made the free choice between the alternatives on offer. Indeed, the determining grounds may themselves provide the motives behind the courses of action on offer but it is the will which decides between them.[2] Titius emphasizes this when he says that the choice is the "spontaneous inclination of your will" but Caius still seeks to escape the closing jaws of the trap by claiming that even his choice was necessitated. Titius counters that with "this inclination of the will, far from eliminating spontaneity, actually makes spontaneity all the more certain, provided that 'spontaneity' is taken in the right sense" (ibid.).

Kant has clearly cast himself here as Titius and makes three significant assertions in the one passage below. He gives us: (i) his definition of spontaneity (spontaneity "taken in the right sense"); (ii) his definition of freedom; and (iii) his unequivocal stance on freedom. In passing, we can also note that Kant, with (ii), is foreshadowing the apparent paradox presented in the *Groundwork* of the exercise of freedom through obeying a law.

> [i] For spontaneity is action which issues from an inner principle. [ii] When this spontaneity is determined in conformity with the representation of what is best it is called freedom. The more certainly it can be said of a person that he submits to the law, and thus the more that person is determined by all the motives posited for willing, the greater is that person's freedom. [iii] It does not follow from your line of argument that the power of antecedently determining grounds impairs freedom. (Ibid.)

Titius, having been previously concerned to deny Caius the solace that he was necessitated in his bad actions, then goes over to the offensive, seeking to undermine Caius's own stance as philosophically unsustainable stating that "I am going to show you the silent deception which creates in you the illusion of the indifference of equilibrium" (*NE*, 1:403). His tactic is to show that true equilibrium does not exist and that we "strive towards objects in conformity with our desire but also . . . interchange the reasons themselves in a variety of ways and as we please."[3] Our ability to do that, states Titius, is shown by the fact "we can scarcely refrain from supposing that the addressing of our will in a given direction is not governed by any law or subject to any fixed determination." To demonstrate the presence of the desire which determines our will, Titius suggests a thought experiment where a course of action is chosen but then we turn "our attention in the opposite direction." For Titius, the strength of feeling against taking this opposite course shows the strength of the original inclination. *Ergo*, there is no true equilibrium with nothing to disturb it. Will as the power of choice determines which course is adopted. For Kant, it is this power of choice which demonstrates our freedom. To this he adds an additional supporting argument. Should there be true equilibrium without disturbance, subsequent actions would be random (cf. *NE*, 1:402) and this would negate moral responsibility as effectively as would necessitation. Henry Allison advances the same reading, interpreting Titius/Kant as follows, and endorsing *New Elucidation*'s significance in the development of Kant's thought on freedom:

> Kant's claim that the notion of a lawless will involves him in an absurdity places him squarely within the metaphysical tradition that rejects the conception of a "liberty of indifference." This rejection is a constant in Kant's thought; it can be found in his earliest significant discussion of freedom,[4] where he defends the Leibnizian view. (1986, 400)

Caius, however, does not give up so easily and re-raises the awkward topic of God's foreknowledge. This issue was shown earlier to have the potential to undermine any seemingly workable theodicy. The reason for this, granting for argument's sake that God is not the author of evil, is an omniscient God nevertheless still chose to create mankind knowing that evil would be committed. Caius states:

> But I am convinced that you are faced by difficulties which are equally great. In what way, do you suppose, can the determinate futurition of evils, of which God is in the last analysis the ultimate determining cause, be reconciled with his goodness and holiness? (*NE*, 1:403)

God seems to be in trouble when Titius appears to agree:

> It seems that He cannot persecute the sins . . . with all the anger to which the holiness of His nature entitles Him, since the blame for all these evils eventually redounds upon God himself, as the one who first engineered their occurrence. (Ibid.)

Titius gives even further ground when he refers to a series of interlinked events that include both moral and physical evils:

> *God initiated a sequence of events.* This sequence, in the fixed connected series of interlinked, interconnected and interwoven grounds, *embraced even moral evils*, as well as the physical events corresponding to them. (*NE*, 1:404; emphasis added)

With these passages the argument between the two proponents seems to have gone a complete circle and led nowhere. The second passage might also suggest that Kant, at this stage of his career still held onto some vestigial link between moral and physical evil despite what he wrote earlier in *Universal Natural History* breaking that link. In my view, this is not the case as Kant uses the term "physical events" not "physical evil." He is merely saying that suffering can result from moral evil which no-one would dispute. This suggestion concerning moral evils is also close to Alexander Pope's position in his *Essay on Man* which was highlighted when Reflection 3704 was discussed but which would be eventually rejected in the later *Only Possible Argument*. Despite these apparent setbacks, Titius believes that he still can "dissipate the clouds" for Caius as he also states that "it does not follow that God can be accused of being the Author of morally corrupt actions" (ibid.). Titius holds that if we were mere machines with no option but to passively carry out pre-established functions the accusation against God would stand but he re-asserts his claim of self-determination and freedom (cf. *NE*, 1:404).

It is significant that here Kant is offering a description of human freedom[5] as a means of absolving God but is not yet able to explain how it is that we are free. Indeed, nine years later but still in his pre-Critical period, in the 1764 work *Inquiry concerning the Distinctness of the Principles of Natural Theology and Morals* Kant acknowledges this situation when he states that "even today the philosophers have not yet succeeded in explaining the concept of freedom in terms of its elements, that is to say, in terms of the simple and familiar concepts of which it is composed" (*DP*, 2:282).

However, despite the unconvincing dialogue summarized above, what matters for present purposes is whether Kant himself was sufficiently convinced of the reality of human freedom at the time of writing despite the lack of a conclusive explanation or deduction. I contend that he was and thus another of the pre-conditions for offering or defending a theodicy is met. It can also be remarked, in fairness to Kant, that he did not have the philosophical toolkit available to him to complete the job in a more satisfactory manner. He had not yet attained one of the crucial insights of his Critical philosophy in his resolution of the third antinomy in the first *Critique* (cf. A448–51), namely that we are free in the intelligible world yet sensibly determined. Indeed, when we see the inconclusive results of his thinking here, it can be seen as part of his working through the problems of speculative metaphysics in general the eventual rejection of which led to his critical, Copernican turn.[6] Indeed, Theis goes further holding that it was through his considerations of theodicy *überhaupt* that Kant was able to crystallize his thoughts on the speculative metaphysics with which he struggled in his pre-Critical period. Theis states:

> We think that it is through the question of optimism and of the critical exercise with regard to Leibniz that Kant intended to put to the test some of the ontological, metaphysical and theological assumptions which registered in his personal

program of reform of metaphysics such as he proposed during the course of the Fifties. (2009, 157; author's translation)

In that connection, it is ironic to note that Kant's first words in *New Elucidation* are: "I am about to throw some light, I hope, on the first principles of cognition and to expound in as few pages as possible the product of my reflection on the subject." It was to be another twenty-six years before Kant was sufficiently satisfied with his efforts in this area to produce the eight hundred plus page first edition of the first *Critique*.

Nevertheless, we must still ask whether Titius's statements constitute an effective rebuttal of Caius's stance on God's foreknowledge. I would argue that it does not. They still do not show how God in creating the world has not also created the opportunity for evil which could have been avoided had He not chosen to create. This was the principal challenge from the argument from Crusius noted earlier. To my mind, this question dogs all Kant's consideration of theodicy without a successful riposte ever being given. Kant never provided a rebuttal to the charge of complicity in evil that, through His foreknowledge, God knew that evil would occur but nevertheless He still chose to create. The only apparent solution would be to remove the element of choice from God and claim that the concept <God> included the idea that God MUST create and thus any supersensible being which did not create was not God. It must be stressed, however, that Kant never put forward such an argument.

ON WHAT FOUNDATION DOES KANT'S POSITION THAT THERE IS A GOD REST?

In the introduction, it was stated that the existence of God must be a live proposition for someone concerned with theodicy. It was for the pre-Critical Kant and the best way of confirming this is to examine his consideration of God's attributes and the arguments for His existence in the period in question. It is well known that in the first *Critique*, Kant dismisses the three, and, for him, the only three possible[7] theoretical proofs of God's existence (A590–630), and that in the second *Critique* he advances a so-called moral proof (cf. *CPR*, 5:124–25). Kant's stance in his pre-Critical period on the existence of God is part of the story of his move toward this eventual position, but this progression was far from linear. In his early pre-Critical period Kant did not see a need for a theoretical proof of God's existence; it was not required either to support faith or for philosophical purposes. Indeed, in his early work, it often seems to be taken for granted that God exists and further, that Kant appears to accept those attributes of God conventionally assigned to Him in the mid-eighteenth century. For example, in Reflection 3704, Kant makes the following observation on Leibniz's *Theodicy*:

> But, appealing to the goodness, wisdom and power of God which are sufficiently well-known from other indisputable reasons, he [Leibniz] gives such people reason to hope that the defects will be balanced by benefits in the whole. (*Refl*, 17:232)

But Kant does not question God's goodness, wisdom, or power, nor set out the indisputable reasons. In a similar vein, also in Reflection 3704, Kant starts his consideration of Leibnizian optimism (theodicy) with: "[o]ptimism is the doctrine which justifies the existence of evil in the world by assuming that there is an infinitely perfect, benevolent and omnipotent original Being." However, in examining that Reflection, we saw Kant giving an early indication of his concern about theoretical proofs of God's existence and the reliance placed upon them in deriving or accepting the then conventional attributes of God. In consequence, I held that Kant was amongst the "troubled" to which he referred (cf. *Refl*, 17:233). There is one pre-Critical work which Kant devotes to the proof of God's existence, namely *The Only Possible Argument* but the first signs of Kant seeing the need for a proof emerge eight years earlier in *New Elucidation*. In this earlier work, one of the propositions considered by Kant states, "[t]here is a Being, the existence of which is prior to the very possibility both of itself and all things. This Being is, therefore, said to exist absolutely necessarily. This being is called God" (*NE*, 1:395). The basis of his argument is that is that the concept of possibility is grounded on comparison. But, for comparison there must be an existent to compare with and thus "it follows that nothing can be conceived as possible unless whatever is real in every possible concept exists and indeed exists absolutely necessarily" (ibid.). In other words, possibility is grounded in actuality, reality. Thus even what is not now but will be in the future is possible only because there is a necessary being containing all reality, past present and future, and this being we term God. At various points in his argument he presents the corollary, for instance when stating that "if you deny the existence of God, you instantly abolish not only the entire existence of things but even their inner possibility itself" (ibid.). So the first thing that can be said about Kant's pre-Critical God is that it is a necessary being which prevents an infinite regress of determining grounds which suggests that Kant, at this stage of his career, was attracted to what would be later termed the "Cosmological Argument."

The argument for God's existence which Kant put forward in 1755 in *New Elucidation* was in many ways a rehearsal for a refined version of the argument from possibility in *Only Possible Argument* of 1763. This is clear when he states in the latter work that "[t]he argument for the existence of God which we are presenting is based simply on the fact that something is possible" (*OPA*, 2:91). In this view, I am following Manfred Kuehn who states, when describing the argument of the *Only Possible Argument,* that "a rudimentary version of the argument is already present in the *Nova Dilucidatio* [New Elucidation]" (2001, 140). Also L. W. Beck holds that "the *Only Possible Argument* repeats, with a few changes, the modified form of the ontological argument presented already in the *Nova Dilucidatio*" (1969, 455).

Nevertheless, some comment on the title *Only Possible Argument* is appropriate. Its tentative nature, evident from the full title, is significant as Kant explains that his aim is not to provide a demonstration but rather to offer some considerations which could contribute at some stage to this. To me, this indicates that Kant was not confident that what he was about to offer amounted to a sufficiently rigorous, complete proof. Loades has a similar view. She states that "Kant reiterated the point that he could not offer a rigorous demonstration of the existence of the deity but only direct attention to what he proposed was the one source of reality" (1985, 119). Indeed, in the Preface to the work, Kant acknowledges this by means of an analogy with a building. He sees himself as only offering the materials out of which the eventual building (argument for the existence of God) could be constructed. This highlights the tentative nature of Kant's claims in this matter. However, the work's opening sentence shows that he was not at all tentative in a much more important regard:

> I do not esteem the use of such an endeavor, such as the present one, so highly as to suppose that the most important of all our cognitions, there is a God, would waver or be imperiled if it were not supported by deep metaphysical investigations. (*OPA*, 2:65)

In other words, whatever the result of the search for a proof of God's existence, there is no way in which Kant's faith in God would be undermined. Further, it also shows that Kant does not see a proof as required. Yet, by this stage of his career, I maintain that he was caught in an uneasy no-man's land between faith in God which did not require a proof of His existence and his desire as a philosopher for such a proof. This is also evident from his further statement that faith in the existence of God does not require "metaphysical investigations." Despite proofs which meet the demands of common sense, "scholars feel the lack of a demonstration" (ibid.). It is noteworthy that Kant is here discriminating between faith and knowledge as he will famously do in the preface to the second edition of his first *Critique* (cf. Bxxx). He is also stating that it is not a requirement for faith to have the objective certainty which would flow from a metaphysical demonstration. This is the first mention of the different grounds for faith and knowledge which he will expound with his tripartite taxonomy[8] of *Fürwahrhalten*[9] that will become an established component of Kant's moral philosophy in later works, and indeed form one of the pillars supporting his own eventual "authentic" theodicy.

As the purpose here is to illustrate the existence and nature of Kant's belief in God at this stage of his career, a detailed re-examination of the proof from possibility as set out in *Only Possible Argument* is not needed. What is significant for this study is that Kant at this stage of his career was giving it serious consideration. Also significant, despite the work's title, is that in *Only Possible Argument* Kant puts forward a second possible argument of a different stripe in the First Reflection of Section Two, namely "In which the Existence of God is inferred *a posteriori* from the Unity perceived in the Essence of Things."

In this, Kant is once more concerned principally with what he sees as the underlying unity which exists in nature. He supports his argument by probing the opposite case:

> A multiplicity, in which each individual [entity] had its own special and independent necessity, could never possess order, or harmoniousness, nor could there ever be unity in their reciprocal relationships to each other. (*OPA*, 2:95)

He goes further to make the supposition, on the basis of the observed unity, "that there is a supreme ground of the very essences of things themselves, for the unity in the ground also produces unity in the realm of all its consequences" (*OPA*, 2:96). In other words, he is arguing from the unity of the consequences to a single supreme ground. This sounds much like an attempted teleological proof of God's existence but this is different from the *a priori* proof from possibility which forms the major theme of the work (cf. *OPA*, 2:91). This additional argument could also be called a higher-level teleological proof since he is concerned not with the immediate purposiveness of nature but rather with the underlying laws of nature which ground its perceived unity. An argument of this nature is not new, Kant having advanced it previously in Reflection 3704 and in *Universal Natural History* (cf. *UNH*, 1:331).

This consideration of a teleological-type proof on Kant's part is surprising as in the same work, he appears to dismiss teleological (physico-theological) and cosmological proofs when as he states that "[n]one of the proofs which argue from the effects of this being to its existence as cause can ever—even granting that they are of the strictest character, which they are not—render the nature of this necessity comprehensible" (*OPA*, 2:91). If there is now doubt about Kant's position, this would seem warranted as this dismissal occurs earlier in the work *before* the advancement of the higher-level teleological proof discussed above. However, Kant offers us a partial resolution in tabling the Reflection "In which the Inadequacy of the usual Method of Physico-Theology is demonstrated" (*OPA*, 2:116). Here he advocates the supremacy of such a proof based on the unity in nature over a proof based either on miracles or the contingent order of nature. Kant then offers an extended case for his revised Physico-Theological method (cf. *OPA*, 2:117–37) and it would appear that he is advancing a rival argument to that from possibility. But Kant acts to close the emerging fissure:

> Nor, indeed, is the ground of my amazement removed once I have convinced myself that all the unity and harmony I observe around me is only possible because a Being exists which contains within it the grounds not only of reality but of all possibility. (*OPA*, 2:152)

In other words, his revised Physico-Theological argument rests on the antecedent argument from possibility. Nevertheless, despite this perplexing diversion, Kant shows that he has recognized the only corners from which any possible proof of God's existence could emerge and the standard which it must meet:

> All arguments for the existence of God must derive from one or other of two sources: either from the concepts of the understanding of the merely *possible*, or from the empirical concept of the *existent*. . . . What has to be proved, namely, is the existence, not merely of a very great and very perfect first cause, but of the Supreme Being who is above all beings. (*OPA*, 2:155)

In the above I have discussed the possible proofs of God's existence thematically but, when reordered chronologically, a different picture emerges from a high level *précis*:

1. 1753. In Reflections, 3703–5 Kant's discussions are based on the assumption that God exists.
2. 1755. In *New Elucidation*, Kant advances a prototype argument from possibility.
3. 1759. In *Optimism*, Kant's arguments rest on some unidentified stance with respect to God's existence.
4. 1763. In *Only Possible Argument*, despite the title, Kant offers not only a detailed version of the argument from possibility but also considers a dependent physico-theological argument despite a seeming rejection of *a posteriori* proofs.

The challenge for the Kant scholar is what conclusion can be drawn from Kant's consideration of the proofs of God's existence in the pre-Critical period. This is especially difficult in light of the disconcerting and far from rectilinear progress exhibited by points 1 through 4. Although it might seem to be avoiding scholarly responsibility, I hold that there is no need to draw firm conclusions provided my stance is accepted that the pre-Critical period for Kant was a time of exploration, not transition, and certainly not one of final conclusions.

Nevertheless, for the purposes of this study, it is enough that the above considerations fully illustrate Kant's conviction that there *is* a God, something he never lost in his career. Speculation about the strength of that faith would be groundless, but still Kant could not resist the intellectual attraction of emerging theoretical proofs even though he had not embraced the need for them. The final words of *Only Possible Argument* provide a cogent summary of Kant's position: "It is absolutely necessary that one should convince oneself that God exists; that His existence should be demonstrated, however, is not so necessary" (*OPA*, 2:163).

So, in sum, for Kant there is a God and human beings have freedom. As the types of evil to be addressed were identified in the previous chapter, all the prerequisites for a theodicy are now met. This allows examination of those theodicies which Kant in his pre-Critical period saw as successful.

ARE PHILOSOPHICAL THEODICIES POSSIBLE?

It is certain that Kant fully appreciated the work that any theodicy must do. In *New Elucidation*, he discriminates between antecedently and consequentially determining grounds stating that the first explains "why, or the ground of being or becoming" and the second "that, or the ground of knowing" or as he states "a consequentially determining ground does not bring the truth into being" (*NE*, 1:394). But this is no interesting yet abstract move on Kant's part since he applies this differentiation to evil. His move is important for this study since Kant was recognizing here that he had not only to search for a reasoned argument to support a theodicy but also a theodicy has to answer reason's demand for the explanation, the ground, *why* evil can exist concurrently with a moral God. In the Introduction I argued that these were the two demands of reason that a theodicy *must* meet.

As stated at the start of the chapter, I contend that Kant, in his pre-Critical period, did see philosophical theodicies as possible. Assessing the evidence for this is best done in chronological order but when this is done it will be seen that Kant's stance yet again does not follow an orderly progression. Also, it must be stressed that at no point Kant does state "here is my theodicy" or similar. Rather, the evidence consists in statements that imply a theodicy because they offer the reasoned explanation recognized as needed (cf. *NE*, 1:392).

In Reflections 3703–5 Kant showed that he fully understood the nature of Leibniz' theodicy not only with respect to the best possible world but also the distinction between God's antecedent and consequent will. Nevertheless, there is nothing in these Reflections to support a claim that he explicitly endorsed Leibniz's theodicy. Indeed the opposite would seem to be the case since in Reflection 3705 he raised the two significant problems discussed in chapter 1. Whilst these problems were solved later we should not look for an unambiguous endorsement of Leibniz as Kant's stance on theodicy at this stage of his career. Rather in Reflection 3704 he expressed his preference for Pope's system (cf. *Refl*, 17.233).

Whilst I hold that Kant failed to differentiate sufficiently between Pope's system and that of Leibniz, what matters here is Kant's attitude to the former. Pope's system does not deny that things, injurious to humans, happen in this world but claims that everything, of whatever nature, is for the good—"whatever is, is right." That Kant endorses Pope's system and claims that everything gives expression to God's perfection is to offer a theodicy in all but name, since what is experienced as evil serves a higher purpose to a greater good. In the following year, 1755, Kant gives us the following in *New Elucidation*:

> By thus pruning away the branches which yield an abundant harvest of evils, and, in so far as it is compatible with human freedom, eliminating them, He has in this way shown Himself to be someone who hates all wickedness, but also someone who loves the perfections which can nonetheless be extracted from that source. (*NE*, 1:405)

In the one sentence, Kant is contemplating three quite different genres of theodicy. First, when he underscores human freedom he is suggesting a free-will defense of God. Such a defense claims that, in giving humans the freedom needed to be morally responsible, it is unavoidable that some will misuse that freedom to commit evil and that God is not to blame for such misuse. In this way, moral responsibility and moral evil are the opposite sides of a single coin; you cannot have one without the other. Second, eliminating all avoidable evil is presumably directed toward producing or maintaining a best possible world. Finally, the idea that good or "perfections" can be derived from evil suggests an instrumental account of evil or greater good theodicy. Kant also put a greater good theodicy into the mouth of Titius in the imaginary dialogue: "God also allowed things to creep into his scheme which, in spite of the admixture of many evils, would yield something which was good and which the wisdom of God would elicit from them"

(*NE*, 1:404). Indeed, a free-will defense could be interpreted as a greater good theodicy as it can be claimed that God in foreknowledge chose to create a world containing free human beings knowing that the good which would come from that would more than outweigh the evil that He foresaw. Whilst Kant did not explicitly make such a connection, in the passages above, there is ample evidence that in 1755 Kant believed that philosophical theodicies could be successful.

One cautionary note is needed. In the conclusion of the second Earthquake Essay, Kant again sketches the outline of a greater good argument when he states that "That same supreme wisdom...has subordinated lower purposes to higher ones . . . to attain those infinitely higher aims that far surpass all the resources of nature" (*EE2*, 1:460). This suggests that Kant considers that the undoubted human suffering which results from natural disasters might be somehow serving a divine higher purpose which is unknown to us. At first sight this looks like a theodicy. However, as Kant has explicitly rejected natural harm as a form of evil, to be consistent, this cannot be a theodicy as there is no evil involved.

In 1759, Kant wholeheartedly defended the best possible world in the *Optimism* essay which was a source of later embarrassment to him. Whilst his defense is unquestionable, he does not endorse a theodicy based upon it even though he recognizes that is how Leibniz has employed the concept (cf. *Opt*, 2:29). But is that enough to argue that Kant was not advancing a theodicy, despite the lack of an explicit endorsement of Leibniz? I judge not. If one states that the world is the best possible that God could have realized, whether through limitations in His power or those from compossibility and simultaneously acknowledging evil's presence in the world in general, then one is inescapably excusing God from at least partial responsibility for that residual evil. In the previous chapter, Kant's later embarrassment about *Optimism* even in his pre-Critical period was highlighted which could suggest some back-tracking on his part with respect to the best possible world. I take that not to be the case since any embarrassment could have arisen from (i) the realization just four years later with *Negative Magnitudes* that evil was not just that resulting from limitation but there was also evil with a positive ontological ground, and (ii) his toe-curling praise of the best possible world at *Opt*, 2:34–35.

Although in the *Only Possible Argument* of 1763 there is much on the laws of nature, there is little in the way of an implied theodicy. However, as we have seen, Kant offers an interesting perspective on God's conjectured intervention in these laws through miracles (cf. *OPA*, 2:112). Namely, if God acted through miracles to bring about a perceived improvement in the world, it would be an admission that the world was not the best possible in the first place. Thus best possible world theodicies are lent significant, but perhaps unintended, support by Kant's rejection of miracles at this stage in his philosophical career.

In sum, during his pre-Critical period Kant saw philosophical theodicies as possible and gave evidence of this at several points in his writings. Whilst he entertained possible theoretical proofs for God's existence, he had yet to reach the point with the first edition of the first *Critique* where he rejected them. A corollary of these possible proofs being accepted is the claim, at least implied, to have at least some knowledge of God. That the theodicies of this period were based on such knowledge of God did not at this stage invalidate them in Kant's eyes. In the next part of this study dealing with the early part of his Critical period we will see this picture beginning to change.

NOTES

1. Hereafter *New Elucidation*.
2. Schönfeld (2000, 158) comments on this passage that "the will is the master, the motive is its servant." In this way Kant is advancing the opposite of the famous Humean position where reason is the slave of the passions.
3. This anticipates the "natural dialectic" Kant describes in the second *Critique* in which we attempt to rationalise making ourselves an exception to the moral law in order to follow our sensible inclinations.
4. Allison footnotes a reference to *New Elucidation* 1:398–405, the same section being considered here.
5. David Walford, whose translation is being used as the primary text here, points out in a footnote that Kant later rejected the account of freedom given here, citing, *inter alia*, the second *Critique* (*CPR*, 5:95–101).
6. For a thorough treatment of this rejection, see Schönfeld (2000).
7. Thus, by implication, also dismissing his argument from possibility in *Only Possible Argument*.
8. Opinion/belief/knowledge.
9. Holding-to-be-true.

Part II

THE EARLY CRITICAL PERIOD
A Time of Transition

INTRODUCTORY REMARKS

The start of the period saw the publication in 1781 of one of the seminal texts in the history of thought, *Critique of Pure Reason*. Whilst this revolutionary work was marked by Kant's famous Copernican turn, I will show that with respect to theodicy at least, his thoughts developed in a more measured way.[1] It will be seen that for Kant in this period there were some pre-Critical holdovers, some definite changes from that period, and the first discussions of some aspects, such as God's role in morality, that point forward to the third time period, late-Critical, and the substantive treatment they receive there. For these reasons, study of this period is essential if a full account of the development of Kant's thought on theodicy is to be given. Indeed, such a study illustrates the gestation of Kant's definitive stance on issues the significance of which extends far beyond just theodicy. So it is not enough to just present the start and end points of his consideration of the subject. The major sources upon which this part of the study draws are the first edition in 1781 of the *Critique of Pure Reason*, the work which ever since has defined the watershed in Kant's philosophy, and the *Lectures on Philosophical Theology*. These will be supplemented by two shorter works considering history from a moral philosophical perspective: *Idea for a Universal History with a Cosmopolitan Aim* (1784)[2] and *Conjectural Beginning of Human History* (1786).[3] But first the scene must be set.

NOTES

1. Some scholars, for example, Frederick Beiser and John Silber, do talk of a Copernican turn in Kant's moral philosophy. This is based on a claimed parallel, the reversal in this case being that of the right and the good when Kant argues in the *Groundwork* that the moral law precedes the good rather than following from it.
2. Hereafter *Idea*.
3. Hereafter *Conjectural Beginning*.

Chapter 4

Setting the Scene

JUSTIFICATION OF THE USE OF *LECTURES*

Before considering how Kant's thought on theodicy evolved in his early-Critical period, it is essential to justify any reliance on *Lectures* as caution is warranted with this source. The reason for such caution is that *Lectures* was not published until 1817, some thirteen years after Kant's death, based on notes taken by his students in lectures given in 1783/4, some thirty years previously. Various other lecture notes taken by Kant's students were worked up into book form with Kant's approval in the last decade of his life, but *Lectures* is not one of these. It is thus without his *imprimatur* which gives rise to three specific concerns.[1] The first is whether *Lectures* accurately reflects Kant's then current views. The second is that lecturers at Königsberg University in Kant's time were required to lecture to set texts, in this case Baumgarten's *Metaphysica*. This prompts the question "does *Lectures* reflect Kant's views or those of Baumgarten?" The third concern is the divergent views in the literature on the standing of *Lectures*.

A sample of four views illustrates this last concern. Amongst those taking a positive view is Christopher Insole in his 2008 paper "The Irreducible Importance of Religious Hope in Kant's Conception of the Highest Good." In this he relies heavily on *Lectures* to support his arguments. That he does so without questioning *Lectures*' reliability suggests that he is not concerned on this score. A second supportive view comes from Duncan who considers *Lectures, Conjectural Beginning*, and *Idea* as a group to show the agreement between *Lectures* and the two published works from the same period in which the *Lectures* were given (cf. 2012, 975n). Set against these positive indicators, two negative ones. In his book *Kant as Philosophical Theologian*, Bernard Reardon cites Gerhard Lehmann, the editor of the *Akademie Ausgabe* of *Lectures,* as being "somewhat dubious of the full authenticity of the Pölitz text [*Lectures*] as it stands" (1988, 76), suggesting it is an amalgam of three other partial texts. This in turn suggests that an extra editing process could have taken place to fuse *Lectures* into the single text we know today. The concern is that each editing cycle is another interpretative exercise potentially taking the eventual result further from the original. Another reservation comes from Karl Ameriks. In his *Kant's Elliptical Path,* he includes the following view on *Lectures*: "[t]he most detailed indication of Kant's view on God's metaphysical relation to us comes from some not *clearly* trustworthy notes to lectures on philosophical theology, apparently from the 1780s" (2012, 275; emphasis in original). However, Ameriks's words suggest to me, not that *Lectures* must be disregarded, but rather that *Lectures* cannot be given the benefit of the doubt and must be regarded as untrustworthy until proved otherwise. Such a conservative attitude toward a source of doubtful authority is fully warranted until a satisfactory level of justification can be provided. I intend to put forward such a justification and this will contain three strands. They are showing that (i) Kant was prepared to disagree with Baumgarten in principle, (ii) Kant disagreed with Baumgarten in *Lectures* on matters specifically connected to theodicy, and (iii) Kant's views in *Lectures* are indeed consistent with those in *Idea* and *Conjectural Beginning* as argued by Duncan.

Disagreement with Baumgarten in Principle

A clear example is to be found near the start of first *Critique* in the first part of the Transcendental Doctrine of the Elements which Kant terms the Transcendental Aesthetic. In this, Kant shows that space and time are *a priori* forms of intuition. Thus he gives "aesthetic" a different meaning to the conventional one of his time, and this forms the grounds for disagreement with Baumgarten:

> The Germans are the only ones who now employ the word "aesthetics" to designate that which others call the critique of taste. The ground for this is a failed hope, held by that excellent analyst Baumgarten, of bringing the critical estimation of the beautiful under principles of reason, and elevating its rules to a science. But this effort is futile. (A21n)

That Kant was prepared to use the words "failed hope" and "futile" to characterize the efforts of one of the period's foremost philosophers and to reserve the word "aesthetic" for his own epistemological purpose[2] illustrates significant disagreement. It is not necessary, however, to rely on just

Lectures on this issue. For example, in *Metaphysik Herder*, Kant considers that Baumgarten did not define cohesion correctly (cf. *LM* 28:46). Further, in *Metaphysik Mrongovius*, Kant states that Baumgarten's ontology "is a hodgepodge <*farrago*>, gathered up knowledge which is not a system" (*LM* 29:785). All this provides, in my view, reliable evidence of Kant's readiness to challenge and disagree with Baumgarten where he felt this was justified.

Disagreement with Baumgarten on Theodical Issues

The next challenge to using *Lectures* arises from the requirement that lecturers at Königsberg University had to use set texts, in this case Baumgarten's *Metaphysica*. Again, this could lead to the charge that the views put forward in *Lectures* were not Kant's own but those of Baumgarten. Whilst Kant did indeed use that work, I contend that it was not to teach from but rather to act as a foil for his own views. To support this, we have Kant's own statement at *Opt*, 2:35: that "[i]n the coming semester, I shall, as usual, be lecturing on ... metaphysics and ethics using Baumgarten." Offering a modicum of support to my contention is Kant's use of the word "using" not "from" but unsupported by further evidence, reliance on just this one word would be unwise. However, Kant disagrees with Baumgarten at several places on matters relevant to theodicy, but two examples involving God's properties suffice here.

First, *Lectures* records Kant as stating that "[i]f the author talks about God's *sincerity*, this expression is far beneath the dignity of the highest being" (*Lect*, 28:1084), noting that "author" refers to the author of the text Kant is using, namely Baumgarten. Here Kant is taking issue with Baumgarten[3] as he (Kant) holds that attributes such as sincerity are only "negative perfections" in the sense that someone would predicate of them of God only for the purpose of denying them. Kant holds that anyone who in that way would deny God's sincerity would no longer be talking about God. Additionally, Kant gives us to understand that attributes such as truth and sincerity are secondary qualities which can be subsumed under "holiness," one of God's three moral properties acknowledged by him.

Second, Baumgarten offers the following in *Metaphysica* §922 "since God's highest life is absolutely necessary (for it is his essence itself and his existence), God is not only immortal, but *only he has absolute immortality*." Kant acknowledges that God is immortal due to the "absolute necessity of his [God's] existence," but holds that "the expression 'immortality' is unsuitable, because it is only a mere negation of an anthropomorphic representation" (*Lect*, 28: 1089). Kant sees that, despite their representational usefulness, we need to purge our concept of God of such anthropomorphisms. One can infer that Kant's objection to "immortal" was that it referred to an entity as "not dying" but even the denial of death is not part of the concept of God. Kant justifies such an inference when he states that "it is much better to use the expression 'eternal' instead of 'immortal' since it is nobler and more appropriate to the dignity of God" (*Lect*, 28:1089). From these two examples, I maintain that where Kant disagreed with Baumgarten in matters affecting theodicy, he was prepared to say so and such disagreements are reflected in *Lectures*. This conclusion is in line with that of Schönfeld who summarizes the situation as "although Kant's textbook Baumgarten's *Metaphysica* was as conventional as it gets, Kant's comments were not" (2000, 232). Kant was using it as a foil for his own views.

Comparison with Published Material

Whether the notes which led to the *Lectures* were accurate *in toto* cannot be answered but what we can do is to compare Kant's views as recorded in *Lectures* with those in published works of the same period. *Lectures*' reliability in this regard has been attested to by Schönfeld (2000) and Duncan (2012). They argue that views expressed in the two minor works, *Idea* and *Conjectural Beginning*, coincide with those in *Lectures*. Nevertheless, given the essential role of *Lectures* will have in this part of the study, an independent examination of this issue is desirable rather than relying solely on the conclusions of others.

In *Conjectural Beginning* Kant offers an account of Genesis where the "Fall" results from human beings becoming conscious of their power of reason.[4] Before that, human beings were merely animals responsive to instinct and thus incapable of right and wrong. Kant states:

> Before reason awoke, there was neither command nor prohibition and hence no transgression; but when reason began its business and, weak as it is, got into a scuffle with animality in its whole strength, then there had to arise ills and, what is worse, with more cultivated reason, vices, which were entirely alien to the condition of ignorance and hence of innocence. (*CB*, 8:115)

Kant is here treating Genesis at two levels. First, he is clearly ignoring a literal interpretation of the Biblical story with its apples and serpents. Second, he is not dismissing the reality of a fall but it is a fall from pure animality into humanity as a species, a fall from moral ignorance into moral accountability.[5] The corresponding statement in *Lectures* records Kant as saying:

> A special germ toward evil cannot be thought, but rather the first development of our reason toward the good is the origin of evil. And that remainder of uncultivatedness in the progress of culture is again evil. Is evil inevitable, and in such a way does God really will evil? (*Lect*, 28:1078)

The agreement here between these passages concerning evil's origins, the first from 1786 and the second from the notes taken in 1783/1784 requires no amplification, but there is another element in the second citation which demands attention. This is the notion of progress toward the good. Again, agreement with this can be found in *Conjectural Beginning*:

> Whether the human being has gained or lost through this alteration [the development of reason] can no longer be the question, if one looks to the vocation of his species, which consists in nothing but a *progressing* toward perfection. (*CB*, 8:115)

This agreement is strongly reinforced by the continuation from *Lect*, 28:1078 where Kant gives an early indication of a three phase development: first man as animal, then man who uses reason to work out the way achieve ends given to him by his inclinations, and then, finally, man uses reason for its own sake with the potential for the good/perfection.[6] Additionally, with his statement that "[e]vil is also not a means to good," Kant is distancing himself from the instrumental theodicies which we saw him contemplating in his pre-Critical period.

The theory of the origin of evil through growth in reason but which at the same time held out the prospect of eventual perfection is also to be found in *Idea*. Kant presents the work in eight propositions. The second begins "in the human being (as the only rational creature on earth), those predispositions whose goal is the use of his reason were to develop completely only in the species, but not in the individual" (*Idea*, 8:18). Kant is here confirming that the development of reason occurs in not the lifetime of each individual (i.e., in Man rather than in a man) but rather a gradual trans-generational development from animal through human to full rationality (see *Idea*, 8:20 and *Lect*, 8:115–16).[7] The three way match we now have between *Lectures*, *Conjectural Beginning*, and *Idea* on this important topic acts not only to increase the confidence that the first properly reflects Kant's views but the re-examination has also unearthed theodically interesting material. In particular the idea of the growth in reason will be reconsidered later to determine whether such an account of moral progress grounds a theodicy or not.

So to sum up, I hold that the foregoing analysis shows that (i) Kant was prepared to disagree with Baumgarten when this was needed, (ii) in the lectures he gave Kant was prepared to disagree with the content of Baumgarten's *Metaphysica*, and (iii) views expressed in the *Lectures* do coincide with those in published works from the same period. With such a foundation in place, it is now possible to mine the theodically relevant material in *Lectures* with confidence. Reinforcing this conclusion is the agreement to be found between *Lectures* and the first *Critique* on various topics. This will be shown in the next chapter when "Innovation" in Kant's early Critical period is considered thematically.

THE FIRST *CRITIQUE* AND THEODICY

It is plainly not my intention here to embark on a comprehensive examination of the first *Critique*, a path already beaten wide by the work of many a distinguished scholar. My aim is more modest, namely to bring under consideration only that material which is relevant to the aim of tracing the development of Kant's thought on theodicy. Experienced students of the first *Critique* might well hold that there is nothing of theodical relevance in that work. In contrast, whilst acknowledging that Kant did not present a theodicy, even an implicit one, and never used that word in the first *Critique*, I hold that there are two important functions that the first *Critique* performs concerning theodicy. One provides in Kant's terms a negative discipline (cf. A795 and below) and another, a positive role.

First, there is the negative discipline. That for which the work is most famous, Kant's revolutionary metaphysics and epistemology, acts to limit the claims of any theodicy which is to remain compatible with these aspects of his thought. Specifically, there are implications from the limitations of our possible knowledge and from Kant's dismissal of the theoretical proofs of God's existence. It will be seen that this is a key factor in Kant's later rejection of philosophical theodicies in *Failure*.

Second, there is the positive discipline. Contained in just thirty pages (in the *Akademie Ausgabe*) toward the end of the work is the second chapter of the Transcendental Doctrine of Method—The Canon of Pure Reason.[8] Here Kant rehearses many of the ideas in moral philosophy which he will fully develop in later works, particularly in the second *Critique*. The most significant of these ideas for this study is that of the Highest Good which is dealt with in the second section of the Canon. This forms the pivot around which Kant's moral faith turns. This second, positive, role will not be examined in detail here as consideration of the topics dealt with in the Canon is better postponed until the thematic treatment covering all the relevant early-Critical works in the following chapter.

The Effect of Kant's New Metaphysics and Epistemology

A major achievement of the first *Critique* was establishing the boundaries of what we could know. In what became famous as his Copernican turn, Kant showed that our senses do not present us with the appearance of the world as it really is but rather that we construct such appearances ourselves. However, this is not reworked Berkeleyean idealism because what we perceive does not owe its existence to our perception. Rather it is grounded in things as they really are, things-in-themselves, to which we do not have epistemic access. In the production of knowledge, the senses are fundamental, necessary but not sufficient as understanding is also required. Sensation is the faculty of representation being affected by an object's presence and intuition is cognition in that sensibility. However, sensibility does not work independently from our cognitive facilities in that each sensation already displays the hallmark of spatial and temporal organization which is imposed by the subject on the raw sensory input. Thus Kant terms space and time *a priori* forms of intuition. The understanding acts to bring the manifold of intuition under categorical concepts, such as causality and substance, also given *a priori*, which provide structure to the manifold and without which our sensory experience would just be a jumble. This knowledge can be used together with existing knowledge organized under concepts gained empirically to reason inferentially. This is an exceptionally abridged description of the path to knowledge, but the essential point for Kant and for this study is that this path starts with the senses[9] and can start in no other way, since the categorical concepts on their own are blind.[10] As a result, we cannot have *knowledge* of what we cannot perceive; there is a boundary to knowledge.

Now, at various points in his philosophy, Kant asserts that, despite the limits of knowledge, it is in man's nature to still seek the grounds for what he experiences; he is an explanation-seeking animal. This process is unending and, viewed as a whole, forms a search for the unconditioned, that without an antecedent ground. Now, for Kant, pure reason is that without empirical content, and so a critique of pure reason is just that, a criticism of the use of reason to claim knowledge beyond its proper boundaries. Kant reminds us of this at the opening of the Canon:

> The greatest and perhaps the only utility of all philosophy of pure reason is thus only negative, namely that it does not serve for expansion . . . but rather, as a discipline, serves for the determination of boundaries, and it has only the silent merit of guarding against errors. (A795)

However, this is does not mean that reason's use beyond the boundaries of knowledge is invalid but what it considers there are *ideas* of pure reason not knowledge. Kant holds that the three principal ideas falling under this stricture are: the freedom of the will, the immortality of the soul, and the existence of God. Now an ideal is an individuated form of an idea, so when Kant talks of God in the first *Critique*, it is as an ideal of pure reason. It is important to note that ideals are not products of the imagination but "even though one may never concede them objective reality (existence), [they] are nevertheless not to be regarded as mere figments of the brain; rather, they provide an indispensable standard for reason" (A569). Whilst at no point does Kant claim that we have (or can have) knowledge of this God, it is clear that a great deal can still be thought about this ideal with Kant, for example, offering that it is "singular, simple, all-sufficient, eternal, etc." (A580).

The implication for any attempted theodicy is clear and quite startling. Any theodicy which relies on claimed knowledge of God whether this is derived by theoretical reason, from a purported divinely revealed text, or simply asserted, must fail in Kant's eyes. This would seem to present an insuperable difficulty for the person, including Kant himself, who attempts to advance any theodicy. Mark Larrimore goes as far as to suggest that the "first *Critique* made theodicy null and void" (2004, 79). But this is to go too far since there is an alternative and better interpretation available. It is that the would-be theodicy constructor must seek another route to God which does not amount to a knowledge claim and yet is robust enough upon which to base a theodicy. It will be seen later that this is exactly what Kant did. Kant confirms this stance with respect to knowledge of God at various places in the first *Critique*. One is enough for present purposes and that included here also has the advantage of indicating the alternative route to God which Kant will eventually take, the moral route:

> [A]ll attempts of a merely speculative use of reason in regard to theology are entirely fruitless and by their internal constitution null and nugatory, but that the principles of reason's natural use do not lead at all to any theology; and consequently, if one did not ground it on moral laws or use them as guides, there could be no theology of reason at all. (A636)

From the final part of the citation we see that Kant was not concerned with theology *per se* but with *rational* theology just as he is concerned later in the second *Critique* to show that it is *rational* faith which is warranted. For Kant, theology and faith must be grounded in reason which is consistent with the pre-eminent role given to reason in his definition of theodicy.

Possible Proofs for the Existence of God

It might be thought that showing that knowledge of God is impossible was sufficient to undermine the extant claimed proofs of God's existence. Clearly, Kant thought he had to go further. He held there were three and only three such proofs and his dismissal of these has been the subject of much scholarly thought. So a short description of each and the reason for its dismissal by Kant will be sufficient here. First, there is the Ontological Proof which attempts to show that the concept of God necessarily implies His existence. The proof attempts to do this by claiming that the concept of God as existing is more perfect than a concept of God who does not exist. By such an argument, as

God is all-perfect, *ergo* God exists. Kant dismissed this proof by famously asserting that existence is not a predicate and consequently existence adds nothing to the concept of God. Existence merely means that the concept is instantiated. It can be noted that this explicit rejection also implies abandoning the tentative *a priori* ontological-type proof from possibility in the pre-Critical *Only Possible Argument* which was discussed earlier. Second, there is the Cosmological Proof. In short, this sets out an argument from existence in general to the existence of a necessary being, one that contains the ground of its own existence, to terminate an otherwise infinite regress. The proof then states that since there is at least one existent, myself, an absolutely necessary being must therefore exist. It purports to be a proof from experience of the world and thus cosmological but Kant dismisses it as merely a disguised version of the ontological proof. This is because something can only exist necessarily if its existence is part of its concept and arguing from the concept of God to His existence Kant has already discounted. Finally, there is the Physico-Theological Proof which instead of considering existence in general, "uses observations about the particular constitution of this sensible world of ours for its grounds of proof" (A605). As we have seen Kant was attracted to this final proof but only in providing a focus in studying nature[11] and an intellectual foundation for the order that is perceived there. Nevertheless, Kant ultimately dismisses it too. He concedes that all it could ever establish would be a highest architect of the world but never a creator of the world.[12] Indeed, Kant holds that in attempting to move from world architect to creator, the physico-theological proof makes an appeal to the cosmological proof which in turn is only a concealed ontological proof. Again, it can be noted that this also invalidates any tentative proof from experience which I argued was also present in outline in *Only Possible Argument*. The outcome is that Kant holds that we cannot prove the existence of God through theoretical reason but, equally, the corollary is that theoretical reason cannot prove His non-existence either. As far as theodicy is concerned, any attempt which employs similar reasoning or a call on the results of these proofs is therefore bound to fail if it is not to conflict with the kernel of Kant's Critical philosophy.

With the preliminary issues now dealt with and the scene set, the way is now clear to move forward to the detailed consideration of the topics related to theodicy in Kant's early-Critical period.

NOTES

1. For the history of the material which formed the *Lectures*, see the Editor's Introduction in *Religion and Rational Theology* (337). In the editor's view, the lectures that formed the basis of the *Lectures*, were given in 1783/1784.

2. Kant revisits this whole subject in 1790 with his third *Critique* when he offers a Critique of Aesthetic Judgment where "aesthetic" has a more conventional meaning.

3. The editors of *Religion and Rational Theology* highlight the following in n68 (p. 480) from Baumgarten, *Metaphysica* §919 as the proposition Kant is opposing: "SINCERITY is benevolence concerning what is signified in one's mind, and this is in God."

4. Christine Korsgaard (1996, 110) offers the same reading.

5. It is a fall at an individual level too when the age of reason is reached—the age at which a child is held capable of discerning right from wrong.

6. Kant develops this idea of a three-phase development fully in the *Religion* of 1793.

7. This is a Darwinian rather than Lamarckian moral evolution where this would take place in the individual—the phenotype.

8. Hereafter "Canon."

9. This is not an endorsement by Kant of Humean empiricism, which is without the logically prior structuring provided by forms of intuitions and categorical concepts.

10. A51: "Without sensibility no object would be given to us, without understanding none would be thought. Thoughts without content are empty; intuitions without concepts are blind."

11. Because of the argument's usefulness in the study of nature which displays such order, Kant will recast the argument as physico-*teleological* in the third *Critique* thus divesting it of any theological significance.

12. In *Universal Natural History*, Kant's support for the ongoing functioning of the laws of nature made, in my view, the role of a highest architect redundant; all that was needed was the initial materials and the laws of nature.

Chapter 5

Aspects of Theodicy

The objective of this chapter is to substantiate my characterization of Kant's early-Critical period as transitional. As highlighted before, such a transition is in marked contrast to the revolutionary change which occurred in his metaphysics and epistemology with the 1781 publication of the first *Critique*. I will argue that Kant's theodical thought shows that different components of his overall philosophical project were developing at different speeds and hence got out of step with each other. My stance rests on an examination of theodically relevant topics drawn from the four primary sources listed in the previous chapter but foremost amongst these is *Lectures*, which underscores the importance of the earlier justification for its use. These topics have been gathered into three groups as an elucidatory device only, the boundaries between the groups being occasionally fuzzy. The three groups are: (i) topics where Kant's thought is unchanged from his pre-Critical period; (ii) those where there is a clear change; and (iii) those appearing in his thoughts for the first time and thus innovations.

EARLY CRITICAL CONTINUITY

In this group there are five topics where I consider that Kant's thought was maintained, broadly unchanged from his pre-Critical period, but which continued to be relevant to theodicy in the period under consideration.

The Continual Workings of the Laws of Nature

In examining his pre-Critical period, we saw repeated assertions by Kant that there were universal and unchanging laws of nature that were continual in operation, with no exceptions for time, place, or person. Additionally, this stance was strengthened when Kant embraced Newtonian mechanics as the description of these laws. However, in the resultant system, Kant still kept a place for God but not as the "hands-on" manager of the universe. In *Lectures* Kant's commitment to the principle of no detailed management of nature on God's part is again apparent. He states that "[i]t would be presumption, and a violation of God's holy right, to want to determine precisely that this or that is and had to be God's end in the production of a certain thing" (*Lect*, 28:1069). Our earlier consideration of *Universal Natural History* and *Only Possible Argument* showed that Kant downplayed, if not rejected, miracles and this is also continued in *Lectures*, when he not only reinforces the point concerning detailed management but also regards miracles as undermining order in the world (cf. *Lect*, 28:1109). This would be not only because general rules would not be followed but also if God intervened in every act there would be no rules at all.

Notwithstanding his position on God's intervention, whether routinely or by means of miracles, Kant continued to resist any suggestion that the continual working of the laws of nature without divine intervention in any way diminished God and reduced Him to a deist God, stressing this point as:

> But if we find that a great deal of the order and perfection in nature has to be derived from the essence of things themselves according to universal laws, still in no way do we need to withdraw this order from God's supreme governance. (*Lect*, 28:1070)

This is clear evidence of Kant's continuing desire to keep a place for God within an essentially Newtonian physical world and within his philosophical system *überhaupt*. When this topic was discussed in the earlier examination of the *Universal Natural History*, we saw that Vailati made the useful distinction between an interventionist God and conservationist God. In these terms, whilst Kant continues to reject the notion of a God who continually intervenes in the workings of the universe, this does not mean that He fails to conserve it in its present state. God still exercises supreme governance. This is important theodically since, if God had withdrawn completely from the world after its creation, a "hard" deist view, there would remain a much diminished challenge for theodicy to meet, perhaps none at all since God would be completely divorced from all subsequent events in the word including the evil ones. In his pre-Critical period Kant also used the principles of Newtonian mechanics to defeat the notion of physical evil. The latter, reclassified in this study as natural harm, could therefore never be construed as punishment for moral evil. Thus by maintaining his stance on the laws of nature, Kant also carried forward this important conclusion into and through his early-Critical period and indeed into the late-Critical one.

The Dismissal of Lazy Reason

In *Lectures,* this is a corollary of the continual working of the laws of nature. The dismissal of lazy reason was a recurring theme in Kant's pre-Critical period and one that he saw as the tendency to give up too early searching for accounts based on the laws of nature. When this happened people prematurely stopped investigating the sensible world for explanations and assigned responsibility for phenomena to a divine being. We saw Kant expressing himself in this way in *Universal Natural History.* In *Lectures* Kant is still advising his auditors against lazy reason, stating that "I must nowhere appeal directly to God whenever I perceive beauty and harmony. For this is a kind of lazy reason" (*Lect,* 28:1071).

Although Kant puts the term to a quite different use in the first *Critique,* it nevertheless supports its use in *Lectures* as a warning against unjustified ways of thinking. He states that "the first mistake that arises from using the idea of a highest being not merely regulatively but (contrary to the nature of an idea) constitutively, is that of lazy reason (*ignava ratio*)" (A689). The context in which Kant is setting this particular warning is when one starts to consider the highest being constitutively, hypostasizing God considered as an ideal. There is then a risk that we assign powers and attributes unjustified by *theoretical* reason when, as shown in the first *Critique,* we do not (and cannot) have knowledge of God. However, there is an interesting contrast here. Whereas in *Lectures* Kant was warning against giving up thinking prematurely when phenomena were arbitrarily deemed as God's work and thereby discouraging scientific investigation, in the first *Critique* he is warning against taking thinking too far. This affects theodicy by reinforcing the strictures on claiming knowledge beyond the boundaries of experience which was highlighted in the previous chapter. The reflection here on the highest being as constitutive as opposed to regulative is not the final consideration of the topic. In the following chapter when unresolved tensions are discussed, it will be re-examined in greater depth.

The Happiness of Evil Men

In Reflection 3703, Kant questioned whether the evil man suffered disadvantages in this world to offset the benefits from his evil-doing and whether this might assuage the sense of injustice felt by the upright man (cf. *Refl,* 17:229). In *Lectures* Kant maintains this stance that "[i]f we investigate this closely we find that the disproportion between the two is not really so large. We must not be blinded by the outward glitter that frequently surrounds the vicious person" and "[t]he restlessness of his conscience torments him continually" (*Lect*, 28:1081). This could be construed as a sort of theodicy since it supports the idea of justice in the world, or maybe better as an "anthropodicy"[1] as it does not involve God *per se*. It seeks, however, to reassure the good man that there is some justice in the world after all because the evil man is not as happy as he might seem due to his private turmoil. By 1791 in *Failure*, Kant had completely reversed his standpoint on this. Nevertheless, even if this is an "anthropodicy," it is still significant for theodicy because, if it is correct that evil-doers do suffer in the way Kant still believed they do at this stage of his career, it at least reduces the force of any claim of injustice against God.

Man's Freedom as a Pre-Requisite for Morality

In Kant's pre-Critical period and particularly in *New Elucidation* we saw him concerned to show that man is free to make (im)moral choices. There he rebutted necessitation as advanced by Crusius and, through an imaginary dialogue, put forward an account of freedom, albeit unconvincing in my view. As Kant maintains throughout his career that freedom is required for moral responsibility and so for morality itself, it comes as no surprise that he should express himself in that manner in the period under consideration. For instance, "the human being acts according to the idea of freedom, he acts *as if he were free, and eo ipso he is free*" (*Lect*, 28:1068). However, this is not just confirmation but also a reference to the nature of freedom. In the first *Critique* Kant has shown that we cannot have knowledge of freedom, only an idea of it and the citation from *Lectures* is consistent with that. It also anticipates the move in the third section of the *Groundwork* where Kant again equates acting under the idea of freedom with being free.

The Best Possible World

This topic illustrates the sometimes fuzzy boundaries between the groupings adopted. Nevertheless, the inclusion of this topic here is warranted because the end-result was the same, namely that Kant in the period in question, in my view, continued to support the notion of a best possible world, our world. However, the grounds for such support began to expand to also encompass moral ones. The starting point is Kant's continuing support in *Lectures* of the best possible world, which he had so staunchly defended in Leibnizian terms in the 1759 *Optimism* essay:

> That the world created by God is the *best* of all possible worlds is clear from the following reason. If a better world than the one willed by God were possible,

then a *better will* than the divine will would also have been possible. (*Lect*, 28:1097)

In addition to this theological defense of the best possible world, where God is an entity that per definition always chooses the best, Kant also supports another of Leibniz's arguments for such a world. This is that we are not in a position to judge the whole of Creation (world in this context comprising more than our planet). Hence, we cannot state that this world is not the best possible despite the occurrence of evil. Kant concurs with this limited view of Creation:

If God commands something for which we cannot understand the reason, then this is because of the limitations of *our* cognition, and not because of the nature of the commandment itself. (*Lect*, 28:1114)

This passage, however, does not yield a theodicy but only a defense. Any attempted theodicy based on our "limited view" leaves us unable to judge whether this is the best possible world and in consequence unable to deny that it is so. Such an agnostic state on this matter leaves us unable to acquit or convict God on any charge of responsibility for evil in the world. Thus this argument only defends God rather than offering the reasoned explanation which would meet Kant's definition of theodicy. However, in supporting a "limited view" defense here, Kant still has to walk a fine line, as above we have already seen him continuing to condemn "lazy reason." So care must be taken that the limitations of our view do not come from a failure to think about and explore theodicy energetically. There can be no "lazy theodicy." Once more, in the passage Kant anticipates a key consideration in his late-Critical thoughts on theodicy, namely the ways in which God's *modus operandi* are incomprehensible to us.

However, Kant also introduces another possible ground, a moral one, for supporting the notion of a best possible world, stating:

[F]or if I cannot be sure that the laws governing the course of nature are the best ones, then I must also doubt whether in such a world true well-being will eventually be combined with my worthiness to be happy. But if this world is the best then my morality will stand firm. (*Lect*, 28:1098)

This argument links the best possible world with morality for the first time. It requires that the world is the best possible in order to underpin morality rather than attempting to show that the world is the best possible *per se*. To my mind, such an argument does not work. From Kant's view that best possible world is required to underpin morality it does not follow that this is actually the best possible world. An unsupported requirement on its own cannot form a proof. The passage also includes the notion "worthiness to be happy." Here it is linked with "true well-being" without our being told what such well-being consists in. In the final section of this chapter, where those topics new to Kant's thought will be set out, it will be seen that "worthiness to be happy" is a vital consideration concerning the Highest Good which plays a pivotal role in Kant's late-Critical moral philosophy. Nevertheless, Kant's thinking on the best possible world now has both physical and moral dimensions. However, before ending this consideration of the best possible world, there is a lingering cause for concern which has the potential to place the subject amongst the unresolved tensions to be considered in the next chapter. The concern arises from the following puzzling statement:

> [I]t is possible to recognize the doctrine of the best world from maxims of reason alone, independently of all theology and without its being necessary to resort to the wisdom of a creator in proof of it. (*Lect*, 28:1098)

Kant then argues that the best possible world can be derived from observing nature where "in every plant and animal there is not the least thing which is useless and without purpose" and then claiming that if this is the case with "irrational nature" how much more true it must be for the "nobler part of the world, in rational nature." The impact for theodicy is that with this claim Kant appears to be trying to establish a best possible world without calling on God. This could be a device to exonerate God for evil in the world. Should such an interpretation be correct, it would distance God from His Creation in a quasi-deist fashion. However, it also would leave some doubt about the motivation to establish in such a way that this world is the best possible. Leibniz clearly wanted to show this to be able to defend the justice of God in the light of evil in the world. But here, as there no suggestion of a demiurge-type being at work, Kant seems to be toying with the idea that the world, independently of God, could have made itself the best possible in some way. It would be possible to counter, that since the laws of nature that "every plant and animal" obeys ultimately come from God, there is no problem. However, Kant seems to rule out such response by stating "without its being necessary to resort to the wisdom of a creator." To my knowledge, Kant does not explore this intriguing idea further at any point in his corpus.

The Significance for Theodicy

Although there was no change in these five topics considered, they remain significant for potential theodicies. In summary, they are:

- Any harmful results of the laws of nature are not evil; neither are they divine punishment for moral evil.
- When thinking about God and His attributes, giving up prematurely on explanations for phenomena in the sensible world and seeing their direct causation by God is "lazy reason."
- The injustice arising from the apparent happiness of the wrong-doer is not so great.
- Man carries moral responsibility for his freely chosen evil actions.
- This world is the best possible which God could have chosen to create.

Together, these are limits that would have constrained any formal theodicy that Kant could have put forward at this stage of his career. It should again be noted that Kant does not put forward an explicit theodicy in this period but I hold that these considerations nonetheless have a direct bearing on any search for an attempted reasoned explanation which lies at the heart of a theodicy as identified in the Introduction.

EARLY CRITICAL CHANGE

In this section, two important aspects are examined where the degree of change from Kant's pre-Critical period is sufficiently marked to indicate a distinct break, illustrating the development in his thinking on theodically relevant issues.

Reason and Moral Development

One argument put forward in justifying the reliance on *Lectures* as an authoritative source for Kant's stance on theodicy in his early Critical period was the match between views in *Lectures* and the published works from the same period, *Idea* and *Conjectural Beginning*. One such match concerned Kant's view at that time that the growth in reason in human beings explained the origins of evil as moral evil. Kant states that "[a] special germ toward evil cannot be thought, but rather the first development of our reason toward the good is the origin of evil" (*Lect*, 28:1078).

Here there is a foretaste of Kant's later description of the predisposition to the good in *Religion* where there are also three stages of moral development set out, albeit described in different terms (cf. *Rel*, 6:26–28). It is noteworthy that Kant foresees a time "[w]hen the human being has developed himself completely, evil will cease of itself." The issue is given added potency with this passage from *Lectures*:

In this earthly world there is only progress. Hence in this world goodness and happiness are not things to be possessed, they are only paths toward perfection and contentment. Thus evil in the world can be regarded as *incompleteness in the development of the germ toward the good*. Evil has *no special* germ. . . . It is nothing beyond this, other than incompleteness in the development of the germ to the good out of uncultivatedness. (*Lect*, 28:1078)

Here there are several forward-looking elements: "there is only progress," "paths toward perfection and contentment," and "development . . . out of uncultivatedness," which together prompt questions about the historical process of moral improvement which Kant clearly sees occurring. There are four such questions. First, is the evil which is undoubtedly present in the world we experience serving some purpose? Second, is this evil to be excused as some unavoidable side-effect of a pre-established historical process leading to moral perfection? Third, following on from that question, is God involved as the process director? And lastly, is there a possible theodicy implied, in that evil can be excused because it is either (i) unavoidable due to part of a historical process and/or (ii) instrumental in producing ultimate moral perfection? Should the last be the case, it would be what I have termed elsewhere a "greater good" theodicy. All these questions demand a deeper look at what Kant is recorded as saying on this matter in *Lectures*.

The first issue which can be settled is that Kant undoubtedly sees a historical process in progress. In the above citation there is a persisting Leibnizian tone in Kant's words when classifying evil as a byproduct since, for Leibniz, God does not intend evil through His antecedent will but it still occurs as a consequence. Set against this, with his statement in the continuation that "evil is . . . not a means to the good" (ibid.), Kant is again eliminating any potential instrumental theodicy in which the evil is excused because it produces the good. However, its allowance as a byproduct whilst not being instrumental is quite a fine distinction for Kant to maintain on God's behalf.

When the moral development process is considered, Kant says enough to reasonably conclude that he does not see the process occurring in individual human beings, but rather in humanity as a species. If that should be granted, Kant still leaves it open whether the process is sustained by human effort or whether God is involved and further whether there is some kind of moral historicism at work which inevitably leads humanity toward a predetermined telos of moral perfection. Whichever answer is correct, there are implications for theodicy. In the first case since man is responsible for the pace of progress, individuals would be responsible for the extent of the residual moral evil and this would act as the foundation for a variant of a free-will theodicy. Nevertheless, God's residual responsibility would again seem to be that He chose to create, with the foreknowledge arising from omniscience, a world containing men who would choose moral evil during such a progression. In the second case, the process has been initiated by God in the act of creation. It is outside our control so that humans could no longer be held accountable for the evil. It could even be said in such a case that moral evil *per se* did not exist since this requires human accountability at an individual level to be *moral* evil. A species cannot be morally responsible. What is clear is that the would-be theodicy constructor would then have a well-nigh impossible job to establish God's innocence.

Whichever is the case (or perhaps neither) Kant sees God as exonerated since he states that "[t]his justifies God's holiness, because by following this path the whole species of the human race will finally attain to perfection" (*Lect*, 2 8:1079). Although Kant does not use the word "theodicy," this is one in all but name. One aspect of the agreement between *Lectures* and works published in the same period was that in *Conjectural Beginning* Kant also advanced a "theodicy by progress." In that work Kant again explained that the process started when reason was acquired by humans to accompany their animality and the resultant scuffle between them.

> Whether the human being has gained or lost through this alteration [the development of reason] can no longer be the question, if one looks to the vocation of his species, which consists in nothing but a *progressing* toward perfection[.] (*CB*, 8:115)

One aspect of this historical account, consistent with that in the later *Groundwork,* is that Kant describes how the moral law derived from our rational nature can be in conflict with the inclinations which come about from our sensible nature. None of the above, however, helps to answer the principal question to be addressed here, whether man is in control of this process or merely the input to it, namely what is processed. But whichever is the case, Kant cannot and will not allow any diminution of man's responsibility for moral evil since he states in *Conjectural Beginning*:

> [H]e must not blame providence for the ills that oppress him...he is also not justified in ascribing his own misdeeds to an original crime of his ancestral parents.... [He must] attribute the responsibility for all ills arising from the misuse of his reason entirely to himself. (*CB*, 8:123)

Whilst he accepts the notion of a "Fall" (cf. *CB*, 8:115 and above), Kant is here rejecting the Christian idea of an original sin from such a fall being passed from generation to generation. This rejection means that from the awakening of reason, however basic, Kant holds that man as an individual is responsible for moral evil done and he re-emphasizes this responsibility *ab inititio* when he again assigns moral responsibility to man in this historical process:

> As soon as the human being recognizes his obligations to the good and yet does evil, then he is worthy of punishment because he could have overcome his instincts. And even the instincts are placed in him for the good; but that he exaggerates them is his own fault, not God's. (*Lect*, 28:1079)

So, from the evidence so far, whilst Kant is advancing the notion of a historical process of moral improvement, he remains firm in his conviction that man rather than God is in control of the process, and hence responsible for any progress made and the residual evil which remains to be eliminated. One example of a "process" is the use of the inherent conflict in society for purposes of moral development, Kant stating "the means nature employs in order to bring about the development of all its predispositions is their *antagonism* in society, insofar as the latter is the end the cause of their lawful order" (*Idea*, 8:20; emphasis in original). Kant's argument is that this antagonism takes the form of "*unsocial sociability*" by which he means the tension arising from man's natural tendency to move from an individual existence to one in society and the conflicts that then occur. That is uncontroversial enough when viewed anthropologically or sociologically but the same cannot be said of Kant's assertion about these conflicts when viewed from a moral standpoint. He sees these conflicts "driven by ambition, tyranny and greed to obtain for himself a rank among his fellows" (*Idea*, 8:21) but serving a constructive purpose in the development of man's talents which eventually result in society becoming a "*moral* whole." Indeed, Kant thinks that without such conflict we would remain in an undeveloped Arcadian pastoral life with human beings being hardly better than their sheep. Moreover, "without them [conflicts] all the excellent natural predispositions in humanity would eternally slumber undeveloped" (ibid). Such an argument would clearly provide the foundation for an instrumental theodicy where evil was the means to an eventual good but this is at odds with Kant's prior position that that evil is also not a means to the good. This evolutionary, developmental, account also prefigures a modern Irenaean theodicy of the type termed by John Hick "soul making" in his influential *Evil and the God of Love* (cf. Hick, 2007, 253–61) where this comes close to explaining evil as instrumental in leading to an eventual good state.

So the problem remains how can evil be concurrently a means to the good and inadmissible for such a purpose. A possible way of removing this contradiction is to interpret Kant as holding that evil is not a means to the good for the *individual* but is so for man as *species* in a development process put in place by God. However, such a solution only acts to bring back God's role under the spotlight, especially when Kant concludes this Fourth Proposition from *Idea* with:

The natural incentives to this, the sources of unsociability and thoroughgoing resistance, from which so many ills arise, which, however, impel human beings to new exertion of their powers and hence to further development of their natural predispositions, thus betray the ordering of a wise creator. (*Idea*, 8:21)

This suggests that, whilst an individual man may not use evil as a means to the good, God may do so. Should that be the case, then God would appear to be at least an accessory to evil's presence in the world. At first sight, this appears to make theodicy impossible. However, the above *is* a reasoned explanation but perhaps not one which is appealing to those whose God has the three moral attributes of holiness, goodness, and justice endorsed by Kant. Moreover, there is a possible counter available to God's defender. God provides the good part of the account—the competitive drive and man the bad parts—unsociability and resistance. *Conjectural Beginning* supports this, namely that God is working at the species level, man at the individual level and so can still be held responsible for the committed evil. Competitive drives *per se* are not wrong; man is responsible for their use in an evil way, and therefore God is not guilty of using evil as a means to the good. Such an interpretation is lent support by the citation from *Lect*, 28:1079 above. But it does raise the worry that God and man play by different moral rules, something that firmly rejects in his late-Critical period in a number of works including *Groundwork* and *Failure*.

Free Will Defense

Free will defense is a common theodicy. It takes the general form that God could not have granted human beings free will and at the same time guaranteed that such free humans would not choose evil rather than the good. Thus God is not responsible for humans' evil actions. Indeed, a free will defense can be regarded as a natural outcome, the other side of the coin, of man's moral freedom which Kant asserted throughout his career. Some scholars have responded by attempting to deconstruct the defense by suggesting God could have chosen to instantiate a possible world where humans always freely choose the good, but that will not be treated here. Another common stance, especially in religious circles, is to accept free will defense and to defend it by saying that God in granting man free will made it possible for humans to freely choose to worship Him and not as automata. Whilst in no way reversing his stance on man's freedom or denying a free will defense theodicy *per se*, Kant acts to limit its allowable scope which is a change from his pre-Critical period when there were no such limitations. Kant provides evidence for this at multiple points in *Lectures* and so I hold that there is no question of misplaced reliance on an isolated passage but one citation is sufficient. "[H]e [God] needs no thing external to him, and nothing outside him could increase his blessedness" (*Lect*, 28:1065). Kant is here strongly supporting the stance that God does not need anything from us. Indeed, to be in need contradicts God's perfection and His status as *ens realissimum* and *ens entium*. Accordingly, no successful theodicy can be based on the notion that God wants or needs anything from us. This is not new to theodicy as a subject having previously featured in Leibniz's *Theodicy* where he states that "[i]t is true that we cannot "render service" to him [God], for he has need of nothing: but it is "serving him" in our parlance, when we strive to carry out *his presumptive will*, co-operating in the good as it is known to us" (§58/H155) and "his bliss is ever perfect and can receive no increase, either from within or without" (§217/H264). Thus, whilst the stance was not new, what Kant built upon it was. In his late-Critical moral philosophy he states on more than one occasion that doing God's will is obeying the moral law which is derived from our own rationality.[2] It is not a matter of praising God or seeking His favor, Kant dismissing this as just self-abasement, groveling and wheedling in the hope of reward.

EARLY CRITICAL INNOVATION

There are three important topics with a direct bearing on theodicy which Kant had not examined in his pre-Critical period. They were thus innovations in his thinking. In each of the areas, Kant's thought is of an introductory nature. He will consider them again in his late-Critical period where he builds on the outlines described here to adopt his substantive positions.

The God of Morality and His Attributes

Whilst Kant will later tie God tightly into his moral philosophy, in *Lectures* he starts down such a path in the following way:

> *But our morality has need of the idea of God* to give it emphasis. . . . For if there is a supreme being who can and will make us happy, then our moral dispositions will thereby receive more strength and nourishment, and our moral conduct will be made firmer. (*Lect*, 28:996)

This suggests that Kant had foreseen a role for God in his moral system but that he had not yet reached the position taken in the *Groundwork* that the moral law must be obeyed for its own sake and be driven by no other incentive than respect for it. This need for God in morality is not confined to *Lectures* as Kant had already said much the same in the first *Critique* (cf. A813). Such statements provide ammunition to those who follow Hans Vaihinger's *als ob*—as if, interpretation of Kant's concept of God in his moral philosophy. In other words, acting *as if* there was a God underpins morality. In Vaihinger's view, it is a useful fiction acting as a regulative idea. However, if the above passage from *Lectures* appears to have defined Kant's stance at the time on the issue of incentives to moral behavior, then any certainty does not last as Kant is also recorded as saying "[n]atural morality must be so constituted that it can be thought independently of any concept of God, and obtain zealous reference from us solely on account of its own inner dignity and excellence" (*Lect*, 28:1002).This is much closer to his ultimate stance in the *Groundwork* and the opening of the preface to the later *Religion* (cf. *Rel*, 6:3). However, in the continuation of the above, Kant is recorded as not only reverting to his earlier statement at *Lect*, 28:996 but emphasizing the necessity of the incentive that flows from God's existence.

> But further it serves for this if, after we have taken an interest in morals itself, to take an interest also in the existence of God, a being who can reward our good conduct; and then we obtain strong incentives which determine us to observe moral laws. This is a highly *necessary* hypothesis. (*Lect*, 28:1003; emphasis added)

It is unclear whether Kant is using "necessary" in the sense of "could not be otherwise" or in that of "required" but neither offers a resolution to his seeming indecision. This is further reinforced even when confirming the primacy and self-sufficiency of reason for morality independent of God but nevertheless still wanting to retain some motivational element through His retention in his (Kant's) moral system:

> [T]he duties of morality are apodictically certain, since they are set before me by my own reason; but there would be no incentives to act in accord with these duties as a rational being if there were no God and no future world. (*Lect*, 28:1073)

These apparently contradictory passages are difficult to reconcile. One possible response is that Kant in this period was struggling to establish his definitive position on this issue but that merely leaves the issue hanging in mid-air. Another possible conclusion is that when Kant is talking about self-sufficiency or similar, he is talking about the moral law, *per se*. When he is talking about God's possible role, he is concerned with our motivation to comply with that law, which has yet to reach purity *à la Groundwork*. Nevertheless, Kant is perfectly clear on which element, God or morality takes primacy in his system. It is the latter as is clear from "but moral theology is something entirely different from theological morality, namely, a morality in which the concept of obligation presupposes the concept of God" (*Lect*, 28:1002). Once more cross-reference to the first *Critique* provides the sought-after solid ground:

> Not theological morals; for that contains moral laws that presuppose the existence of a highest governor of the world, whereas moral theology, on the contrary, is a conviction of the existence of a highest being which grounds itself on moral laws. (A632n)

This stance is maintained in *Failure* and in the third *Critique*.

Also in *Lectures*, Kant begins to discuss the apparent tension that will result from the denial that we can have knowledge of God in the first *Critique* (already published in 1781) and yet still be able to postulate a God in the second *Critique*. We are offered a significant clue how Kant will resolve this tension when he refers to what theoretical reason cannot deliver. He states that "for then we would only lack the knowledge that God exists, but a great field would still be open to us, and this would be the belief or faith that God exists. This faith we will derive *a priori* from moral principles" (*Lect*, 28:1010). This last sentence anticipates closely Kant's moral argument for God's existence in the second *Critique*. Further, it is also worthwhile to note that here, and for the first time, Kant is mentioning that the eventual moral proof will be an *a priori* one. These citations also preview Kant's famous assertion at Bxxx in the first *Critique*'s 1787 second edition concerning knowledge and faith. Kant reinforces this idea of another route to God in stating "rather, reason does not put the least obstacle in the way of my accepting the possibility of God, if I should feel bound to do so in another way" (*Lect*, 28:1026). In other words, the failure of the theoretical proofs of God's existence is not to be equated with a proof of His non-existence. Moreover, without such a proof, an alternative route to God still remains open for Kant. It is a moral route to God and forms a *leitmotif* throughout his later philosophy of religion. Kant reinforces this view with the additional consideration that, if we had knowledge of God, then morality would be reduced to merely prudential behavior without moral value, or, looking to the future and the *Groundwork*, imperatives would then be hypothetical not categorical:

> Hence our faith is not knowledge, and thank heaven it is not. . . . For suppose we could attain to knowledge of God's existence through our experience . . . then all morality would break down . . . [since] hope for reward and fear of punishment would take the place of moral motives. (*Lect*, 28:1074)

However, it is possible to interpret the above as further illustrating Kant's indecision on the topic of incentives to moral behavior at this stage of his career. He is here clearly stressing the undesirability of hopes for reward and fears of punishment but what are these other than the possible incentives to obey the moral law which he has seen as needed in other passages highlighted above? Or more colloquially, is this a case of Kant wanting both the penny and the bun?

Before leaving God's role in morality, it is also instructive to look at what *Lectures* can tell us about morality and the theoretical "proof" of God's existence to which Kant was attracted in the first *Critique*, namely the Physico-Theological proof. We are told that:

> [I]f I make into a principle of religion a concept of God such as nature gives me, namely the concept of a very mighty being . . . in short, if I take as this principle not the concept of God as an all-perfect being but only the mere concept of a very perfect being, then from this little or nothing can be deduced toward the confirmation and awakening of a true morality. (*Lect*, 28:1117)

So we can clearly see in *Lectures* Kant confirming the failure of the physico-theological proof to establish an "all-perfect" (as opposed to a merely "very perfect") being. Should the proof nevertheless be accepted, this would cut off the route leading to a God grounded in morality, contrary to Kant's now emerging aim. Indeed, if compliance with the moral law is not to arise from "hope for reward and fear of punishment" because we have knowledge of God, it is *required* that theoretical proofs of God's existence fail. It is also worth restating that one cannot trace the development of Kant's thought on theodicy without also considering the development of his thought on God. Those parts of *Lectures* which have been highlighted are solid confirmation of this.

So if the above looks forward to God's moral role, what attributes must God have in order to fulfill such a role? We will see that God's moral properties are important to Kant's assessment of attempted theodicies in *Failure*. It is therefore interesting to see these emerging in *Lectures* some seven years previously, which adds to the evidence that, in moral philosophy (practical reason), Kant did not experience something like a revolutionary Copernican turn but rather his thoughts germinated gradually. We know already from the first *Critique* that we cannot have knowledge of God. Lack of knowledge, however, does not debar us from having a concept of God and in *Lectures* Kant claims that "[m]orality alone . . . gives me a determinate concept of God" and further that "[i]t teaches me to recognize him as a being having every perfection" (*Lect*, 28:1073). Kant's argument for the latter is that in order to judge whether a person is worthy of happiness in proportion to his moral behavior (in other words, the Highest Good) and to provide that happiness God "must be omniscient, omnipotent, eternal and not in time." In other words, if one grants for argument's sake that Kant succeeds in his argument for God's role in morality, these "omni" properties are those which God must have in order to fulfill it. They result from the demands of morality, not from theoretical reason. This requirement from morality is amplified by Kant's statement that:

> A being who is to give objective reality to moral duties must possess without limit the moral perfections of *holiness, benevolence, and justice. These attributes constitute the entire moral concept of God.* Thus through morality we recognize God as a *holy lawgiver, a benevolent sustainer of the world*, and a *just judge.* (Ibid.)

From this it can be seen that Kant's justification for ascribing these three properties to God is that if any of them were lacking, again we would no longer be talking about a *moral* God.

The Concept of the Highest Good

In Kant's moral philosophy, the concept of the Highest Good plays a central role in that it is used to ground the practical postulates of immortality and God in the second *Critique*. The Highest Good grounds a moral faith in God's existence which does not break Kant's strictures on knowledge of God put forward in the first *Critique*. The importance to theodicy is that it is upon moral faith that Kant bases his own "authentic" theodicy in *Failure*.

Kant first advanced his concept of the Highest Good in 1781 in the Canon of the first *Critique* (A806–10) but did not fully develop it until the second *Critique*. In this later work he defines the Highest Good as virtue (consisting in obedience to the moral law) combined with happiness in the proper proportion to that obedience. In the first *Critique*, whilst Kant does not refer to the Highest Good *per se*, he clearly outlines its two components:

> [T]he necessary connection of the hope of being happy with the unremitting effort to make oneself worthy of happiness [through obedience to the moral law] . . . may be hoped for only if it is at the same time grounded on a *highest reason*, which commands in accordance with the moral laws. (A810; emphasis in original)

Kant also introduces the notion that obedience to the moral law does not comprise mankind's ultimate end, a theme that he will develop fully in the two later critiques. He states:

> Thus without a God and world that is not now visible to us but is hoped for, the majestic ideas of morality are . . . objects of approbation and admiration but not incentives for resolve and realization because *they would not fulfill the whole end* that is natural for every rational being and determined *a priori* and necessarily through the very same pure reason. (A813; emphasis added)

I consider that Kant is making three moves here. First, he is anticipating the practical postulation of God's existence, which he will definitively advance in the second *Critique*. Second, he is, as we have already seen, referring to incentives to obey the moral law other than respect for it but these he rejects in the *Groundwork*. Third, he refers to some "whole end," which is more than obedience to the moral law, and will be eventually specified as the Highest Good.

Lectures, too, contains the building blocks for constructing the Highest Good, albeit not organized into their final form. The first is the worthiness to be happy which also reinforces Kant's stance on the derivation of God from morality:

> Yet on the contrary the concept of God is a *moral* concept, the *practically necessary*; for morality contains the conditions, as regards the conduct of rational beings, under which alone they can be worthy of happiness. (*Lect*, 28:1071)

Kant also adds that to be worthy of happiness but not to receive it involves incoherence, an *absurdum practicum* (cf. 28:1072). Although again not explicitly terming it the Highest Good, Kant provides this excellent description of it:

> Benevolence in and for itself is without limit, but it has to express itself in the apportionment of happiness *according to the proportion of worthiness in the subject*. And just *this limitation of benevolence by holiness* in apportioning happiness is *justice*. (*Lect*, 28:1074)

It is also noteworthy that, in the second sentence above, Kant is setting out the relationship between God's three moral properties, namely holiness, benevolence, and justice. In addition, Kant asserts the pre-eminence of God's justice compared to His other moral properties and expresses this through the application of the Highest Good, stating:

> God himself, the all-benevolent, can make us worthy of his good deeds; but that he shall yet make us partakers of happiness without our becoming worthy of his good deeds in virtue of morality—*that* he, the Just One, cannot do. (Ibid.)

This supremacy of justice is not a transient claim by Kant. He already made it in the second Earthquake Essay and we will see it again seven years later in *Failure*. Yet in *Lectures* the coupling of the concept of the Highest Good with that of God is presented at one point as less intimate than that in the first *Critique* with Kant stating that "God's infinite understanding . . . recognized the possibility of a highest good external to himself in which morality would be the supreme principle" (*Lect*, 28:1102). This opens up the prospect of a possible separation the notion of the Highest Good from that of God which could give rise to a secular Highest Good in this world which avoids endorsing the practical postulation of immortality and God.

In the justification for reliance on *Lectures* reference was made to the correlation between *Lectures* and *Idea* on the subject of the Highest Good. By considering the first *Critique*, we now have a match on this subject between three of our four primary sources which confirms that, with the Highest Good, Kant was deliberating upon a significant innovation in his thinking.

Anticipating the Groundwork

One can regard Kant's moral theology which reaches its apogee in the *Religion* as being built up gradually, layer upon layer, throughout his Critical period. We have already seen how he has already started to consider the Highest Good in the first *Critique*. He puts another sod on the dyke in the *Groundwork* where he identifies reason as the ground of the moral law. However, before making that move in that work, he dismisses happiness as a possible ground for the moral law for three reasons: (i) its indeterminate nature, (ii) the likelihood that one person's happiness is not simultaneously possible with another's, and (iii) the fact that, if happiness was mankind's final end, instinct would have made a better fist of it than reason does with its propensity to clash with our sensible nature (cf. *GW*, 4:395). However, these themes were not first aired in the *Groundwork* of 1785; they can be seen two years earlier in *Lectures*, but again not yet fully worked through[3] as indicated by the following:

> In the idea of happiness ... we have no concept of the whole, but rather we *only compose it out of parts. And just for this reason we cannot direct our actions according to an idea of happiness, because such a whole cannot be thought by us.* (*Lect*, 28:1057)

This speaks to the indeterminate nature of happiness. But Kant goes further to suggest that, if we had happiness in this life, we would not need another life (immortality) as he will postulate in the second *Critique* or a God to ensure the correct relationship between morality and happiness. This would be counter to what I hold to be a fundamental objective for Kant, namely securing a place for God in his philosophical system. This passage also provide an early indication that this correct relationship (the Highest Good) is a matter for the future, intelligible, world not the present, sensible, one.

> If moral duties were only based on feelings, or on the prospect of happiness—so that just by fulfilling them I would become happy already, not merely worthy of happiness ... then well-being would already exist in the present course of things

as the effect of good conduct and I would not need to count only on a happy state in the future[.] (*Lect*, 28:1072)

It is important that here Kant is dismissing duties motivated by the prospect of happiness. Yet he is arguing that Highest Good obtains when the degree of virtue (obeying the moral law) and happiness are in the proper proportion. To dismiss the prospect of happiness as an incentive yet include it in the Highest Good without being an incentive is an extremely narrow path for Kant to tread.

Various passages which anticipate arguments contained in the *Groundwork* have already been highlighted in this chapter but there is one section in particular (*Lect*, 28:1099–100) where Kant rehearses two key moves he will later make in greater detail. First, consider: "For a good will is something good in and for itself, therefore something *absolutely* good, everything else is only a conditioned good" (*Lectures*). Compare this with "It is impossible to think of anything at all in the world, or indeed even beyond it, that could be considered good without limitation except a good will" from the *Groundwork* (*GW*, 4:393). In seeing harmony between these passages, I am following Duncan who states:

> Despite the fact that the *Lectures* predate the *Groundwork* we find Kant saying almost exactly the same thing about the nature of the unconditional good in the *Lectures* as he does in the *Groundwork* and he connects this idea of the will as unconditionally good to the purpose of the world. (2012, 975)

Second, consider "but morality, through which a system of ends is possible, gives to the rational creature a worth in and for itself by making it a member of this great realm of all ends" (*Lectures*). This clearly anticipates Kant's exposition in the *Groundwork* of the second formulation of the Categorical Imperative which assigns intrinsic worth to every rational being and the third formulation which explicitly includes the concept <kingdom of ends>.

In sum, Kant introduced three major innovations in this period of transition which all came to full bloom in his late-Critical period. Although he had yet to demonstrate the rational foundation of the moral law, he had started to link his concept of God with morality, in particular showing how the notion of God flows from the moral law and not the reverse. He began his consideration of the Highest Good, the eventual results of which will enable him to put forward his own "authentic" theodicy. Lastly, the outlines of some the key arguments to be presented in the *Groundwork* have begun to emerge. That the eventual system of morality that will be laid out in that work is based on our rational nature rather than our sensible one will also serve to guide Kant's distinctive efforts in theodicy.

Taking the three sections of the chapter together, we have seen that Kant's thought on topics pertinent to theodicy were subject to development in his early-Critical period. Whilst not abandoning significant aspects of his pre-Critical stance, he nevertheless changed his view on other aspects and provided valuable first insights into yet other matters which will be central in the final period to be considered in this study—the late-Critical. Regarded as a whole, the early part of the Critical period was indeed a time of transition for Kant on theodically relevant topics.

NOTES

1. I thank Georg Cavallar (1993) for this helpful neologism.
2. In other places of his late-Critical corpus, Kant refers to God as the moral law personified and as acting on the laws of morality as divine commands.
3. A view shared by Duncan (2012, 976).

Chapter 6

Pulling the Strands Together

In the previous chapter, the transitional nature of Kant's thought on theodicy was illustrated. But arising from these considerations, there are two questions of consequence which must be addressed. In chapter 3, I argued that in his pre-Critical period, Kant regarded philosophical theodicies as possible. So is that still the case? I will argue that it is. Further, whilst I have described the period presently under consideration as one of transition, toward what is it a transition? In other words, although Kant's thoughts are undergoing change, can we yet see their destination, or, indeed, do they cohere sufficiently for a destination to be identified at all? On this, I will argue that, whilst a general movement toward morality-based philosophy can be discerned, no destination can yet be identified and, further, that there are significant unresolved tensions in Kant's theodical views. The aim of this chapter is to fully address these two important questions.

IS PHILOSOPHICAL THEODICY STILL POSSIBLE FOR KANT?

It is no secret that Kant, in his late-Critical period with *Failure*, rejected philosophical theodicy *in toto*. I contend that in this early-Critical period, in contrast, Kant continued to see such theodicies as possible. That he did not reject them in this period raises or reinforces two broad areas of importance.

First, Kant's change in stance on philosophical theodicy did not coincide with the Copernican turn in his epistemology. Whilst significant for this study, this is not a new claim in the literature, having been advanced, for example by Christophe Schulte (1991) and Duncan (cf. 2012, 973) who points out that *Lectures, Conjectural Beginning,* and *Idea* all post-date the

Copernican turn. As will shortly be seen, there is much material in these works not only to support the stance that Kant still regarded philosophical theodicy as possible and but which also illustrates the range of theodicy types that he still saw as feasible.

Second, the effect of this time lag in his change of stance on theodicy appears to be in conflict with Kant's Critical epistemology since the theodicies which Kant appears to still support rely, at least in part, on knowledge of God which Kant in the first *Critique* asserts is impossible. This aspect will be explored in the following section of this chapter where unresolved tensions from Kant's early-Critical period are considered. Both points demand that my contention that Kant saw philosophical theodicy still as feasible in his early-Critical period be substantiated.

We have already seen in the citation from *Lect,* 28:1079 that Kant argues for a best possible world on the basis that what is better chooses better. As there is, or can be, no being better than God, the world He chose to create cannot be improved upon. To endorse the notion that our world is the best possible despite the presence of moral evil is to imply a theodicy, namely that this world is the best that God could have instantiated from amongst all the possible worlds contemplated by Him. Thus God is not responsible for the unavoidable residual evil in the world. In addition, Kant is reinforcing his position with the secondary argument that, if a better world was indeed possible, then the creator of our world could not be the entity which contains all perfection or reality and therefore not God. In that case, some other kind of "odicy" than a theodicy would be needed.

Also in *Lectures*, Kant offers two further short reflections on theodicy. First, he praises the astronomers who have shown that our world is but a part of a much greater whole. This enables him to advance what I have previously termed a limited view theodicy, or more strictly speaking, a limited view defense. Despite the conflict with the passage above, Kant is recorded as saying that "if our terrestrial globe were the whole world, it would be difficult to know it to be the best and to hold this by conviction" (*Lect*, 28:1097). But because the astronomers have "taught us modesty" regarding our knowledge of the entirety of Creation, it is possible to defend God by taking the line that, despite the acknowledged evil in that part of Creation known to us, it is possible that Creation *in toto* is still the best possible. However, this is a defense of God rather than a full theodicy as the argument advanced cannot acquit God of responsibility for evil in Creation. It only shows that we do not know enough to convict Him either. Second, exceptionally briefly, Kant toys with the idea that "on this earth the sum of pain and the sum of good might just about balance each other." If he had persisted with this line, a theodicy which sought to excuse God for evil because the net effect of good and evil was zero or positive would have been possible. Kant revisits such a calculus later in *Failure*, but only to dismiss it and any theodicy based thereon.

Additional support for theodicy in *Lectures* occurs at *Lect*, 28:1098 (cited previously). This clearly endorses a Leibnizian best possible world but what is striking is that Kant presents it as a demand of reason. Moreover, in the continuation, Kant ties this best possible world to natural science. The latter part of the passage is a description of the Highest Good but Kant is seemingly undermining it by making it dependent on this world being the best possible. This is a risky move on Kant's part because if it could be established that the world is not the best possible, then the Highest Good and all that depends on it in Kant's philosophy would go out the window if this line of thinking was carried through to its conclusion.

In the previous chapter, under the heading "Early Critical Change," the relationship between man's growth in reason and his responsibility for moral evil was fully discussed. Whilst there is no need to revisit that discussion in detail, it is still worthwhile to underscore the outcome. This was that Kant, in effect, was putting forward a "moral progression" theodicy. Kant envisaged a historical process occurring which was put in place by God but man was nevertheless responsible for the evil committed during his progress toward moral perfection, not the "wise creator" who initiated the process. Such a theodicy recognizes that evil occurs but this is discounted because of the eventual result. However, the discrepancy between evil being used as a means to the good by man and its possible use by God was noted. We also saw in the preceding chapter that there was textual evidence for this to be found at *Lect*, 28:1078–79, *Idea*, 8:21, and *CB*, 8:115–16. If such evidence is accepted, Kant was advancing an argument that amounts to a theodicy, but once again, without using that word. Further in *Idea*, with respect to the development of reason, Kant states:

> [T]here will be opened a consoling prospect into future . . . in which the human species is represented in the remote distance as finally working itself upward toward the condition in which all germs nature has placed in it can be fully developed and its vocation here on earth can be fulfilled. Such a *justification* of nature—or better, of *providence*—is no unimportant motive for choosing a particular viewpoint for considering the world. (*Idea*, 8:30)

Here, for Johannes Brachtendorf (2002, 382), Kant is making an explicit appeal to the language of theodicy to describe the development of reason and morality in the species, not the individual. Kant also offers an instrumental theodicy which this time is based on injustice in the world:

> But to sacrifice one's peace, one's powers and one's advantage when the eternal laws of morality demand it, that is true virtue, and worthy of a future recompense! If there were no disproportion at all between morality and well-being in this world, there would be no opportunity for us to be truly virtuous. (*Lect*, 28:1081)

Here, the instrumental role that evil performs is the creation of conditions which demand that we act in a moral way, whether we decide to do so or not. Indeed, Kant is almost suggesting that we could not be moral without injustice in the world. This extract also has the tone that evil can provide the background to make the good stand out more clearly or shine more brightly like a jewel on a dull background. Such a notion is not new having previously been expressed by Leibniz in his *Theodicy* with "[a]nd is it not most often necessary that a little evil render the good more discernible, that is to say, greater?" (§12/H130). Whilst these may not be attractive accounts for some, they are nevertheless reasoned explanations which would meet the requirement for a theodicy as set out in the Introduction.

Kant offers yet another approach to a possible theodicy when he states that "[i]f God commands something for which we cannot understand the reason, then this is because of the limitations of our cognition, and not because of the nature of the commandment itself" (*Lect*, 28:1114). Here, as we have seen before, Kant must tread a fine line. Whilst we cannot prematurely give up our efforts to understand without being accused of lazy reason, this consideration could ground a "limited view" defense. Later, Kant will show in *Failure* that what we cannot do is defend moral evil by calling on a different standard of right or wrong to apply to God.

In considering the evidence presented so far, the reader might not be convinced by my interpretation of the cited passages, namely that they amount to philosophical theodicies or at least provide the bases on which these could be constructed. However, I contend that this is not possible with the final passage now put forward. It is philosophical theodicy pure and simple.

> If . . . God created the whole world for the best, it was necessary to reply to the objection how moral evil could be found in such a best world, then it is now also our duty to show why God has not prevented evil . . . the possibility of deviating from the moral law must adhere to every creature. . . . If the human being is to be a free creature . . . then it must also be within his power to follow or shun the laws of morality. His use of freedom has to depend on him, even if it should wholly conflict with the plan God designed for the moral world. (*Lect*, 28:1113)

There can be no doubt that Kant is here advancing a free-will theodicy with a clearly Leibnizian tone in the final sentence with its implication of the contrast between the antecedent and consequent will of God. However, showing that Kant still advanced philosophical theodicies in his early-Critical period is accepted, this does not end the required deliberations.

UNRESOLVED TENSIONS

The previous chapter dealing with Kant's early-Critical period illustrated its transitional nature. Above, I have argued that successful philosophical theodicies were still possible for Kant. But with those two steps completed, we are still unable to now move forward to consider the third and final period, the late-Critical, as that would be to sweep under the carpet some significant tensions which remain unresolved. They are unresolved in two senses; first Kant does not resolve them and second, I am not able to offer a resolution on Kant's behalf by drawing on the primary material considered thus far in this study. All that can be done for the present is to highlight the issues and note that they must be again addressed when the final, late-Critical, period is considered.

The Nature of Evil

We have seen that in his early pre-Critical works Kant did not contest the prevailing notion of metaphysical evil conceived as limitation, namely that evil is an expression of the shortfall from complete goodness resulting from the limitations inherent in created beings. However, I have argued in Part I that Kant's thought on evil had progressed by 1763 with *Negative Magnitudes*. The interpretation which I offered was that, at that time, Kant put forward an account of evil as ontologically positive, namely as something with a positive ground (a real existent) but with a negative value. However, as he had not rejected evil as limitation by this stage of his career, there were two forms of evil to consider. Such an interpretation, which could also be drawn from *Lect*, 28:1113 above, is challenged at *Lect,* 28:1078 where an apparently unequivocal endorsement of evil solely as limitation would on the face of it preclude any other form.

When Kant's late-Critical writing on theodicy is examined, it will be seen that Kant no longer accepted metaphysical evil conceived as limitation but regarded evil solely as something with a positive ground. Whilst such a stance supports my argument from *Negative Magnitudes*, it does nothing to explain Kant's apparent exclusion here of evil as ontologically positive.[1] One possible move is to abandon my argument based on *Negative Magnitudes* but, as I see no reason to do that, there is a difficulty which cannot be resolved at this stage of Kant's career. Also puzzling is that if evil as limitation is confirmed, God's responsibility for evil increases which is most certainly *not* Kant's intention.

Kant has described these limits as necessary which is correct since creatures *qua* creatures are limited. Taken simply, this means that if man is limited and could not be otherwise, he cannot be held to be morally responsible for evil. Further, if man is not morally responsible, is there any such thing as *moral evil* at all? Should that be the case, the search for a successful theodicy would be moot. No moral evil, no need for theodicy. That a resolution must be found eventually needs no elaboration here since to build a theodicy without settling the question of evil would be to build on sand. This matter will be revisited in Part III (late-Critical) when a solution will be advanced by differentiating between evil and its ground.

The Ontological Status of God

Those familiar with the first *Critique* might query the inclusion of a discussion of God's ontological status at this stage in the study. They could justifiably point to where Kant provides the clearest answer to the question whether the ideal of the highest being is regulative or constitutive. He does so in that part of the Doctrine of the Elements entitled "Discovery and explanation of the dialectical illusion in all transcendental proofs of the existence of a necessary being" (A614–20). It is worthwhile outlining his argument in this matter as it seems to provide a settled view on the ontology of God at the start of Kant's Critical period. The illusion referred to is the hypostatizing of a necessary being and a highest reality which for Kant can only be an ideal of pure reason. Further, the concept of a necessary being sets up a significant dilemma. On the one hand, when something is regarded as existing, then "one can find no way around the conclusion that something [else] also exists necessarily."[2] On the other hand, there is no existent about which we cannot think of its non-being and, for Kant, this results in a situation where "I can never *complete* the existing without assuming a necessary being, but I can never *begin* with this [necessary] being" (A616, emphasis in original). Because of this contradiction Kant holds that neither of these principles can be objective. They can only be "subjective principles of reason" being merely heuristic and *regulative* and this he confirms in the following:

> The ideal of the highest being is . . . nothing other than a regulative principle of reason, to regard all combination in the world as if it arose from an all-sufficient necessary cause, so as to ground on that cause the rule of a unity that is systematic and necessary according to universal laws; but it is not an assertion of an existence that is necessary in itself. (A619)

That would appear to settle the issue. Namely, that for Kant at the time of the first edition of the first *Critique*, the concept of the highest being, God, was a regulatory principle. He saw that it was mistaken to "represent this formal principle ... as constitutive and think of this unity hypostatically." In this way, a regulative principle would be turned into a constitutive one. However, that is not the end of matter when one checks whether Kant adheres to this line later in the first *Critique*. At multiple places later in the first *Critique* Kant does so, again describing the concept of God as a regulative ideal, but one example will suffice here and this, in my view, can only be read in a regulative manner.

> Thus they [the transcendental ideas, which include God] should not be assumed in themselves, but their reality should only hold as that of a schema of the regulative principle for the systematic unity of all cognitions of nature. (A671)

If God as a regulative ideal was Kant's final position on this topic, the challenge in constructing an eventual theodicy would be serious. Irrespective of whether one uses the tripartite Leibnizian taxonomy of evil or the one put forward in this study on Kant's behalf in the pre-Critical Part I, they share the common element of moral evil which must be accounted for in any attempted theodicy where reason demands the reconciliation of such evil with God. If God were to be purely regulative, one would be trying to reconcile existent moral evil with an ideal in a philosophical system. In other words, in such a theodicy one would be seeking to account for evil again as *if*[3] God existed. Alternatively, one could say that no explanation would even be needed since God as an ideal merely sets a unifying standard for moral behavior for humans to live up to. If this line was adopted, theodicy would then be largely redundant. Kant did not attempt to solve such a puzzle at this point in his career and neither do I on his behalf. However, if one puzzle is avoided then another serious one soon becomes apparent because the first *Critique* also contains material which, in my judgment, reads in a realist manner, an example being:

> Hence everyone also regards the moral laws as *commands*, which, however, they could not be if they did not connect appropriate consequences with their rule a priori, and thus carry with them *promises* and *threats*. This, however, they could not do if they did not lie in a necessary being, as the highest good,[4] which alone can make possible such a purposive unity. (A811; emphasis in original)

This is realist in tone because a regulative ideal cannot issue promises and threats. It can also be noted that this passage suggests once more an incentive to obey the moral law resulting from the fear of threats or promise of rewards. These would be classed as hypothetical imperatives in the *Groundwork* a few years later, and so rejected as the moral law's foundation. In that later work the only allowable incentive is respect for the moral law founded on the categorical imperative. The reader could also question whether Kant is here trespassing on territory put out of bounds by his own Critical epistemology since he has shown that we cannot have knowledge of God, yet God seems here to have promise and threat issuing attributes. This realist tone is reinforced at A813 in which Kant appears to be advancing an existent. So despite Kant's explicit assertion at A614–20 that the highest being is a regulative ideal when it comes to applying this outcome in practice, the situation is far from clear and it is here that the unresolved tension lies. We now seem to have two separate concepts of God in play, a regulative ideal (anti-realist) and a constitutive one (realist), namely one for whom some kind of existence claim is being made. Any attempt at a reasoned explanation for the co-existence of God and evil by means of a theodicy clearly requires a stable concept of God. However, in my view, Kant is not providing one at this stage in his career. It will be seen, when his late-Critical period is considered, that Kant resolves this issue when advancing his authentic theodicy.

The Attributes of God
and Their Relation to Critical Epistemology

Having considered God's ontological status and in so doing discussing some possible divine attributes, a wider examination of the latter is worthwhile. But how is God as an ideal to be characterized without making a knowledge claim which is inadmissible following Kant's Critical epistemology? We saw how Kant thought that whilst we could not have knowledge of God we could nevertheless have an idea of God and that in Kant's terminology an ideal of pure reason is an exemplar of such an idea which we would wish to somehow describe. Can these seemingly contrary notions be held onto concurrently?

At the start of the first section of *Lectures*, "Transcendental Theology" (*Lect*, 28:1013), Kant is recorded as laying out "three *constitutive* concepts" of God (emphasis added).

1. God is an original being (*ens originarium*) which is not derived from any other being. Kant considers that this concept of God is the basis of cosmo-theology and "from this concept . . . I infer the absolute necessity and highest perfection of God."
2. God is the highest being (*ens summum*). For Kant this suggests a being with every reality (an *ens realissimum*) and he sees such a being as the foundation of onto-theology.[5]
3. God is the being of all beings (*ens entium*) and is "the highest ground of all other things, as the being from which everything else is derived."

Kant considers that all other "predicates [of] God in what follows ... will only be individual determinations of those fundamental concepts." This is consistent with Kant's criticism of Baumgarten concerning God's attributes which was highlighted previously. Moreover, the third concept is consistent with Kant's reasoning in the *Only Possible Argument* where he held that God could be argued to exist as the ground of all possibility and since what exists is possible, therefore God exists. This link to the argumentation of the *Only Possible Argument* is strengthened when Kant states:

> [W]e can have no insight through our reason into the existence of a being whose non-existence is impossible ... yet our reason urges us on *to assume* to such a being as a *hypothesis which is subjectively necessary for us*, because otherwise we could provide no ground why anything in general is possible. (*Lect*, 28:1063)

However, this apparent linkage to *Only Possible Argument* presents us with a puzzle given Kant's prior rejection in the first edition of the first *Critique* of the three, and to his mind, the only three, theoretical arguments for God's existence. In my view, the puzzle can only be solved if Kant is read as advancing a necessary being as an intellectual focus rather than an existent, again another fine line to tread. Moreover, if this solution to the puzzle is accepted, it would form an argument for a regulative highest being and so we are once more left with Kant advancing both a constitutive and a regulative view of God/highest being in the same work. This was the problem signaled above when considering the concept(s) of God in play in the first *Critique*.

The earlier use of "constitutive" at *Lect*, 28:1013 also raises a significant issue. The constitutive concepts above were set out *after* the publication of the first edition of the first *Critique* where Kant asserts states that we can have no *knowledge* of God. So surely it is a misrepresentation of Kant's position by *Lectures'* note taker to have him setting out *constitutive* as opposed to *regulative* concepts here? In my view, this objection can be accommodated if we interpret what is being advanced as constitutive not of God but of the *idea* of God. In other words, if Kant is read as saying that the idea of God *consists* in these three sub-concepts and that he is not making a knowledge claim that God possesses the attributes. However, an altogether safer approach is not to offer an attempted reconciliation on Kant's behalf at all, especially in the light of his remark:

> Hence the totality of what speculative reason can teach us concerning the existence of God consists in showing us how we must necessarily hypothesize this existence, but speculative reason does not show us how God's existence could be demonstrated with apodictic certainty. (*Lect*, 28:1036)

So, in sum, the unresolved issue here is that, whilst Kant's God is an ideal of pure reason, any description of Him which is required to ground a theodicy seems to require a knowledge which conflicts with his Critical epistemology. One possible explanation for the mismatch is that in *Lectures*, Kant had to trim his sails to the prevailing religio-political wind. However, both Christophe Schulte (1991, 373) and Duncan (2012, 975n) dismiss this possibility by pointing out that the work is based on lectures given late in the intellectually, if not politically, liberal reign of Frederick the Great and therefore before Wöllner's repressive 1788 Religious Edict.

Other Issues

If those are the major challenges, then it is worthwhile briefly recapping the other discrepancies which came to light in the previous chapter. First, when considering the Best Possible World, we saw in *Lectures* (28:1098) Kant appearing to introduce an argument for it which did not involve God. Such an argument would seem to be incompatible with the essentially Leibnizian argument which Kant endorsed elsewhere in *Lectures*. Second, the effect of the development of reason on morality was considered. The possibility was raised there that, whilst man cannot use evil as a means to the good, God might do that when placing in man a spirit of competition which all too often brings man's undesirable qualities to the fore. This re-raised the worrisome question of whether God and man play by different moral rules. Finally, when discussing both the best possible world and God's attributes drawn from morality, the possible incentives to obey the moral law were considered. We saw, at some points in both *Lectures* and the first *Critique*, that Kant stressed the moral law's self-sufficiency and at others, that the concept of God was needed to provide the required incentive to obey the moral law. Is the moral law self-sufficient or not? When added to the three major issues considered above, there is a considerable list of items left to address.

Together, these challenges form a formidable obstacle to any effort to present Kant's thought on theodicy as one of ordered progress. As stated above, I hold that Kant does not provide any convincing answers to these points and neither can I on his behalf. But that would be an unsatisfactory note on which to end consideration of Kant's early-Critical period. When the period is considered *in toto*, what conclusion can be drawn? Whilst I have shown that it was a transitional period with respect to theodicy, we must ask again the question presented in the introduction to this chapter; are Kant's views are pointing toward any specific outcome, despite his move in a general direction toward arguments based on morality? In my view, they do not. Although the pre-Critical period was exploratory for Kant, it is possible to see his position on theodicy as nonetheless relatively ordered. In contrast, at end of the current period, his views appear fragmentary and there are simply too many significant loose ends. The most significant of these is that stated in the introduction to this chapter, namely, that the theodicies which Kant appears to still support rely, at least in part, on knowledge of God which Kant asserts as impossible in the first *Critique*. Epistemology had raced ahead; theodicy lagged behind. The time-lag is not to be explained. It was not just a case of theodicy catching up because Kant had been occupied with other matters. No, in 1783/1784 in *Lectures, after* the publication of the first edition of the first *Critique*, Kant is recorded as expressing views seemingly incompatible with his Critical epistemology. By the end of Kant's career his thinking on theodicy was certainly not fragmented and did not have loose ends. There are two ways in which this shift could have been achieved. Kant could have resolved the ambivalent issues set out here, tying up the loose ends, but he did not. Instead, he rendered these concerns about his early-Critical period redundant by advancing his own unique theodicy which reflected a stable view of God and which did not conflict with his Critical epistemology. Tracing its development and offering a critique of his theodicy's success (or otherwise) forms this study's last major part.

NOTES

1. That Kant is reverting back to an earlier position is also implicitly challenged by Duncan in his 2012 paper in which he argues that Kant made a one-time change from evil as a limitation in 1790 as a result of the work of C. C. E. Schmid when he (Kant) recognized that evil as a limitation of creation would not only absolve Man from evil but place responsibility for it solely at God's door.
2. This is the basis of the cosmological proof for the existence of God.
3. Again, the phrase made famous by Hans Vaihinger (1911) with his *Philosophie des Als Ob* where he saw such a construction as no more than a "useful fiction."
4. Here Kant is referring to God as the "Highest Original Good." When the term "Highest Good" is used in this study without qualification it refers the combination of virtue and happiness in correct proportion.
5. These descriptions match those given in the first Critique (A632).

Part III

THE LATE-CRITICAL PERIOD
A Time of Conclusion

INTRODUCTORY REMARKS

In this third period, Kant adopts his definitive stance on theodicy in *Failure*. He takes an unequivocal position against the philosophical theodicies to which, at least in part, he had previously subscribed. He also advances his own "authentic" theodicy. His last major contribution to the subject of theodicy is made in *Religion* where he sets out his theory of radical evil under which humans are wholly accountable for moral evil, as indeed they must be if any would-be theodicy is to be constructed. In the early part of the Critical period, Kant's theodical thought exhibited unresolved tensions between it and his epistemology but in this late part, with its emphasis on practical as opposed to theoretical reason, these tensions dissipate. They do so not by being addressed individually but by being overtaken by developments in Kant's thought.

Chapter 7

The Failure of Philosophical Theodicies

SETTING UP THE CHALLENGE

It is useful to restate Kant's definition of theodicy. It is "the defense of the highest wisdom against the charge which reason brings against it for whatever is counter-purposive in the world" (*Failure*, 8:255). Although a shorthand version, namely the reconciliation of God and evil, will often be used, it is worthwhile re-emphasizing the full version where it is our *reason* that provides the challenge. Reason's primacy is again stressed by Kant when he describes his examination of philosophical theodicies as a "juridical process ... instituted before the tribunal of reason" (ibid.). Here Kant is referring to his analogy of a trial in which there are four parties. There is God, the defendant, who stands trial on the charge of responsibility for evil in the world. Next there is theodicy's defender or author who strives for God's acquittal, followed by the prosecutor or complainant who wishes to show that theodicies fail. Finally, there is a supposedly impartial judge who will decide on the case purely on the grounds of reason. Also God's defenders cannot "pull rank" on reason by claiming that reason is not fit to judge in matters affecting the divine; in Kant's words "he [God's defender] is not therefore allowed to dismiss the latter [the complaint against God] in the course of the process of law through a decree of incompetency of the tribunal of human reason" (ibid.). Kant's stance here is consistent with that in the *Groundwork* that there is only one moral law, not one for God and one for man. In turn, this is consistent with Kant's insistence on reason's primacy. As there can only be one reason, and the moral law is based on reason, there must be only one moral law.

It is my view that in his examination of philosophical theodicies, Kant is not putting forward his own arguments for theodicies only then to find their defects which would be a rather odd, self-reflective, way of proceeding. Rather, he is reviewing and eventually rejecting various attempted theodicies that were current in his time. As expected, Kant works in a systematic manner. He first identifies three categories of theodicy which its supporters could advance.

a. "Whatever in the world we judge counter-purposive is not so" (ibid.). This is equivalent to saying that what appears as evil is not evil. Clearly, if there is no evil, there is no work for theodicy to do since it has nothing for which to provide a reasoned explanation.
b. "If there is any such thing [as evil], that it must be judged not at all as an intended effect but as the unavoidable consequence of the nature of things" (ibid.). This is immediately recognizable as a key concept from Leibnizian theodicy where, in the best possible world, God does not intend evil *antecedently* but *consequently* permits the evil which results. Further, it was this which underlay the first "serious error" with which Kant struggled in Reflection 3705 as long ago as 1753.
c. "It must be considered not as an intended effect of the creator of all things but, rather, merely of those beings in the world to whom something can be imputed, i.e. of human beings" (ibid.). This is a special case of b. above, but not dealing with the nature of things in general but rather specifically with human beings and their possible moral responsibility. This category also suggests God's consequent permission of evil. It will be seen that, in discussing concrete cases in this category, Kant also considers the nature of evil. However, b. and c. present those who would defend such theodicies with a significant challenge. Namely, to explain how evil is an unintended consequence of God's decision to create but responsibility for it nevertheless does not ultimately attach to Him but rather to those He created.

However, before considering these categories, Kant dismisses two whole classes of theodicy:

> Yet there is one thing he [God's advocate] need not attend to, namely a proof of God's wisdom from what experience of this world teaches; for in this he would simply not succeed, since omniscience would be required to recognize in a given world . . . that perfection of which we could say with certainty that absolutely none other is possible in creation[.] (*Failure*, 8:256)

It is worthwhile making explicit the two classes that this passage excludes. First, Kant is saying that any attempted theodicy based on our experience in the sensible world will fail. Surprisingly, Kant does not explain why at this stage but doing so on his behalf is a straightforward matter. In the first *Critique*, Kant established the boundaries of knowledge and that, whilst we can think of God as an ideal of pure reason, we can have no knowledge of Him. Constructing a successful theoretical theodicy based on our sensible experience would demand reconciliation of that experience with God's attributes and hence a knowledge claim in respect of these attributes. For this reason, such attempted theodicies must *necessarily* fail. Second, we can see that Kant is dismissing any theodicy based on an *a posteriori* claim that our world is the best possible.[1] Here not only are we limited to our sensible experience to debar knowledge of God, but, to compare worlds, we would need omniscience. This we do not possess; only God is claimed to have this property. However, a defense of God, falling short of a full theodicy and thus insufficient for either His acquittal or conviction, could still be attempted based on the limited view which Kant describes.

Kant next introduces two more triads. The first concerns the nature of the counter-purposive in the world which is seemingly "opposed to the wisdom of its creator."

I. "The absolutely counter-purposive or what cannot be condoned or desired either as end or means . . . [this is] the morally counter-purposive, evil proper, sin" (ibid). This is the same as the moral evil from the taxonomy which was proposed on Kant's behalf when his pre-Critical period was examined.

II. "The conditionally counter-purposive, or what can indeed never co-exist with the wisdom of a will as an end, yet can do so as a means . . . [this is] the physically counter-purposive, ill (pain). But now, there still is a purposiveness in the proportion of ill to moral evil . . . namely in the conjunction of ills and pains, as penalties, with evil, as crime" (*Failure*, 8:257). It is important to note that here that Wood and Di Giovanni have used "ill" and not "evil" in their translation. This is exact since Kant uses *Übel* not *Böse*. This supports the argument advanced earlier that Kant, prior to *Failure*, had rejected physical evil as a punishment for moral evil, and indeed, had shown that physical evil is not evil but rather natural harm, or, as here, physical ill. However, two points arise. The first is that it must be again stressed that Kant is not putting forward his own views but evaluating theodicies common in his time and the evils addressed by them. In Kant's time, rejecting the notion of natural harm as divine punishment was far from universal. The second is that there is a potential conflict between Kant's wholehearted endorsement of Newtonian mechanics in his pre-Critical period on which his denial of physical evil was based and the epistemological limits now established in the early-Critical first *Critique*. It will be recalled that Kant adopted these mechanics as the description of the laws of nature put in place by God and then conserved in the universe by Him. Does this suggest that to ascribe this to God is to claim knowledge of Him? I consider that this problem can be discounted if Kant is not claiming to know God as He is but rather recognizing the lawfulness of His action in Creation.

III. "[A] kind of counter-purposiveness must be thinkable in the world, namely the disproportion between crimes and penalties in the world" (ibid.). This is derived from II in that the desired "proportion of ill to moral evil" is absent from the world and this constitutes injustice. However, in *Failure,* Kant in considering injustice, is principally concerned with the negative aspect, namely that the evil escape suitable punishment in this world rather than the positive aspect. The latter is that the proper proportion between obedience to the moral law (virtue) and well-being (happiness) is maintained. This relationship is nevertheless a central concern for Kant which is evident from his consideration of the Highest Good. However, it can be observed that, within theodicy as a subject, this concern with the lack of a proper proportion did not make its first appearance with Kant. Leibniz had clearly recognized this mismatch earlier in his *Theodicy* (cf. §43/H98).

The second triad is God's *moral* properties, namely those which practical reason shows that He must have, not those based on a knowledge claim by theoretical reason. These are unchanged from those Kant which developed in *Lectures* and those set out in the second *Critique* at *CPR,* 5:131n. This means that Kant is making his assessment of philosophical theodicies against the same criteria as in *Lectures,* where he saw such theodicies as succeeding. In contrast, in *Failure* he saw them failing, a crucial turnaround. An important feature of this particular triad, however, is that Kant sets them up, one for one, in direct opposition to the types of counter-purposiveness he has set out in the previous triad. It is for this reason that Kant then proceeds to examine only nine potential theodicies rather than twenty-seven (3^3).

- "[T]he *holiness* of the author of the world, as *law-giver* (creator) in opposition to the moral evil in the world." Moral evil is a would-be offence against God's holiness.
- "[H]is *goodness* as *ruler* (preserver) in contrast with the countless ills and pains of the rational beings of the world." Physical evil (should it exist) is a would-be offence against His goodness.
- "[H]is *justice,* as *judge,* in comparison to the bad state which the disproportion between the impunity of the depraved and their crimes seems to indicate in the world." Injustice in the world is a would-be offence against God's justice (*Failure,* 8:257).

As Schulte (1991, 382) notes, each of these evils is the negative magnitude of the corresponding attribute of God. All other combinations are excluded which means that, for example, Kant does not evaluate moral evil as a possible offence against God's goodness or justice. Whilst such exclusion could be questioned, I will argue later that it proves immaterial to Kant's conclusion. Moreover, it is important to note that Kant considers the three properties to have an order of precedence in application. His argument is that "it is that [o]ur own pure (hence practical) reason determines this order of rank, for if legislation accommodated itself to benevolence, its dignity would no longer be there, nor a firm concept of duties" (*Failure*, 8:257n). This order of precedence matches that previously set out at *Lect*, 28:1073 to which Luca Fonnesu adds the following sharp observation:

> The recognition of holiness as the most important attribute of God agrees with the Kantian conception of ethical religion: holiness characterizes a morally perfect being for whom the moral law is not an imperative but the actual law of his willing and acting. (2006, 768)

THE ATTEMPTED THEODICIES

We can now examine the nine potential theodicies listed by Kant and his responses to them. In addition to offering my own views on these responses, I will be calling on Busche's excellent 2013 paper—"Kant's Kritik der Theodizee—Eine Metakritik," the meta-critique being his critique of Kant's critique of the nine theodicies. Kant identifies the evaluated theodicies by combination of theodicy type and type of counter-purposiveness. This exercise can be usefully presented in a 3x3 matrix.[2]

The first group of three attempted theodicies concerns the disfigurement of the world by moral evil. Should any of them succeed it is doubtful whether there would then be any such thing as *moral* evil to be accounted for. Supporting the taxonomy of evil advanced on Kant's behalf, is his use of the word *Böse*, evil proper, to describe moral evil, not *Übel*, harm. The ability in the German language to make this crucial distinction was commented upon earlier.

Table 7.1 Evaluated Theodicy Schema

	I. Moral Evil vs. Holiness	*II. Physical Ill vs. Goodness*	*III. Injustice vs. Justice*
a. Denial of Evil	Theodicy Ia	Theodicy IIa	Theodicy IIIa
b. Evil Unavoidable	Theodicy Ib	Theodicy IIb	Theodicy IIIb
c. Evil Human Fault, Not that of God	Theodicy Ic	Theodicy IIc	Theodicy IIIc

Ia. In this attempted theodicy it is argued that there "is no such thing as an absolute counter-purposiveness . . . but there are violations only against human wisdom; divine wisdom judges these according to totally different rules, incomprehensible to us" (*Failure*, 8:258). In other words, not only are God's rules and ours are different but also divine purposes could be being served in such a way. Kant also alludes to such reasoning in Isaiah 5:58 when reference is made to "the ways of the most high are not our ways." So the attempted theodicy does not so much try to reconcile moral evil with God's holiness than deny that there is moral evil *tout court*. The strength of Kant's argument against it cannot be assessed because he does not offer one but dismisses it out of hand with a counter-assertion stating that "the vindication is worse than the complaint, [it] needs no refutation; surely it can be given freely given over to the detestation of every human being who has the least feeling for morality" (ibid.). In my view, it is reasonable to judge that Kant saw that allowing this theodicy would make God morally evil to human understanding and this explains his revulsion. Here, however, Kant declines to use two of the weapons he himself has fashioned. First, to accept this theodicy would be to claim knowledge of God's ways in having a different moral system to ours, something ruled out of bounds by the first *Critique*. Second, Kant declined to use the principle of one moral law for both God and man as previously established in the *Groundwork* and which was thus available for his use here in *Failure*. Busche does not see a meta-critique as needed, as, in common with Schulte (1991, 385) and this author, he does not consider that Kant has offered a critique in the first place. Also, Busche questions who amongst theodicy's defenders had put this one forward which to him seems more suitable to defending a tyrant than God. If its defenders are unknown, then Kant was not the first to oppose what lies at the heart of this attempted theodicy, Leibniz having previously stated in his *Theodicy* "nor is it that God's justice has other rules than the justice known of men . . . Universal right is the same for God and for men" (§35/H94).

Ib. In this second "alleged vindication" moral evil is allowed but "it would excuse the author of the world on the ground that it could not be prevented" (*Failure*, 8:259) which is strongly reminiscent of Leibniz's treatment of God's antecedent and consequent will. Kant considers that, if this theodicy were to be granted, then again what appears to be moral evil could not be thus termed as the evil would be an unavoidable part of Creation rather than contingent. Kant's counter-argument is simple but effective, namely that under such circumstances "we would have to cease calling it [the counter-purposiveness] "a moral evil" (ibid.). We have seen Kant distancing himself slowly but surely from Leibniz on theodicy through the two previous periods. But here, although Kant does not make it explicit, his rejection of this theodicy marks another clear break from an important aspect of Leibnizian theodicy, a conclusion shared by Brachtendorf (2002, 72). Kant, however, does not deal with a significant objection to this type of theodicy, that is, that an omniscient God still would have known that unavoidable evil would ensue from His act of creation, albeit indirectly. Yet He chose to create and so must shoulder at least some of the blame for the presence of evil in the world. This is once more the objection put by Caius to Titius in *New Elucidation* and which Kant only rebutted rather than defeated there.

Ic. This attempted theodicy is a variant or special case of Ib. Again, moral evil is initially allowed yet the guilt rests on the human being and not on God "for God has merely tolerated it for just causes as a deed of human beings: in no way has he condoned it, willed or promoted it." Kant rejects this attempted theodicy:

> [T]his rejoinder incurs . . . the same consequence as the previous apology . . . namely, since even for God it was impossible to prevent this evil without doing violence to higher and even moral ends elsewhere, the ground for this ill . . . must inevitably be sought in the essence of things, specifically the necessary limitations of humanity . . . hence the latter can also not be held responsible for it. (*Failure*, 8:259)

Here is the clearest indication that Kant has concluded that if evil flows from the *necessary* limitations of humans as finite creatures, they cannot at the same time be held responsible for the resultant evil in the way this theodicy would portray. Kant cannot accept this as it is a *conditio sine qua non* for him that man, and not God, is responsible for moral evil. Nevertheless, Kant's refusal to accept God's responsibility for evil is not a counter argument just a counter-assertion. However, Kant would again seem to have two good arguments available here but does not make them explicit. First, he is rejecting the notion of a higher purpose which is possible through the allowance of evil. This is sufficient to dismiss the theodicy since it again involves a knowledge claim in respect of God's higher purpose inadmissible under his Critical epistemology. Nevertheless, Kant goes further and rejects the attempted theodicy not on the grounds of claimed knowledge but of evil's necessity. Here I consider him to be mistaken as he appears to equate the ground of the possibility of our doing evil with the evil itself. The former is indeed necessary since our limitations are unavoidable for man *qua* man as created being but this does not make it necessary that evil is committed. In this way, he has another cogent defense available to him with which to argue to his desired outcome of man being responsible for evil but does not deploy it here. Second, in rejecting this theodicy with its talk of "the necessary limitations of humanity" it is also clear that Kant has changed his position on metaphysical evil arising from limitation. This view is shared by Schulte (1991, 387) who contrasts Kant's stance here with that in *Lectures*. Further, Schulte has identified in Kant's *Nachlaß* an exceptionally clear statement of why, for Kant, metaphysical and physical evil must be discounted:

> If everything was based on the sensibility of our nature, then physical or metaphysical harm would be the cause of evil. But then no evil would be our fault but the fault of nature. The accountability rests on the concept of freedom and demands independence from the rule of nature. (23:101; author's translation)

Hence the two-part taxonomy of evil, metaphysical and moral, which emerged from the earlier consideration of *Negative Magnitudes,* is now reduced to a single evil, moral. This important outcome will be examined further in chapter 8 but the significance of this move cannot be overstated. With it Kant significantly updated the concept of evil which he inherited.

Having considered the three theodicies which deal with moral evil contrasted with God's holiness, it is worthwhile drawing up an intermediate balance. A common theme can be seen both in the argument for, and in the refutation of, these theodicies Ia to Ic. First, they either explicitly (as in Ia.) or implicitly (in Ib. and Ic.) point to a higher cosmic purpose to which we are not party in order to justify evil's presence in the world. Kant rightly objects to this type of argument since it excuses moral evil by denying that there is such a thing and therefore there is nothing to accuse God of allowing. Further, if these theodicies were allowed, *Böse* would then be downgraded to *Übel*. Once more, any pretense on our part to know God's higher cosmic purposes would clearly violate the epistemological boundary set by the first *Critique*. Also, whilst the denial of moral evil would be an answer to the Problem of Evil, it would not be a theodicy as this must recognize *both* evil and God before seeking their reconciliation. It can also be noted that these attempted theodicies are *a priori* in nature rather than dealing with the experience of evil. Busche also offers an intermediate balance. He considers Kant's counter-arguments to the three theodicies to be weak but also that there is not enough evidence to convict God. However, in my view, the most important result of Kant's consideration of these theodicies is his rejection of two key aspects of Leibniz's theodicy: arguments from God's antecedent and consequent will in Ib, and moral evil arising from our limitations in Ic. Together, this signals his clear and decisive break from Leibnizian theodicy.

The second theodicy group concerns "the complaint brought against divine goodness for the ills . . . in this world" (*Failure*, 8:259). In considering this group, it is significant that Kant now uses the word *Übel*, harm and not *Böse*, evil.

IIa. This theodicy attempts not so much to reconcile physical ill with God's goodness as to downplay its extent. Such a theodicy has a Leibnizian echo as in the *Theodicy* there is "haply it may be that all evils are almost nothingness in comparison with the good things which are in the universe" (§19/H134). Kant describes the attempted theodicy in the following way: "[i]t is false to assume in human fates a preponderance of ill over the pleasant enjoyment of life,[3] for however bad someone's lot, yet everyone would rather live than be dead" (*Failure*, 8:259), again a view echoing Leibniz's *Theodicy* (cf. §13/H130). We should recall here that, under the categorization system used by Kant, this theodicy is a combination of counter-purposiveness II, physical ill, and theodicy type a, the denial of evil, and hence is supposed to be showing that physical ill is not counter-purposive. Thus the attempted theodicy can only be trying to claim that there is no *net* physical ill. As the theodicy itself does not present an argument as such for this, Kant is surely correct it dismissing it as "sophistry." Busche offers another perspective, considering Kant's response to be weaker than the original theodicy. He considers it to be naive undifferentiated reasoning that is negligent on three counts. First, it is highly problematic that an objective quantification of physical good and ill can be made. Second, should good and ill be able to be quantified and be commensurable after all, man is unable to make such an assessment due to limited view of Creation. This view is again reminiscent of Leibniz who states that "[i]t is thus that, being made confident by demonstrations of the goodness and justice of God, we can disregard the appearances of harshness and injustice which we see in this small portion of his Kingdom that is exposed to our gaze" (§82/H120). Third, Busche holds that a well-founded species-wide evaluation is not possible because of the non-uniform distribution of good and ill among humans. Whilst these three objections are well-made, care must be taken to address them to the correct party, namely, this particular theodicy type and not Kant. As Cassirer (1951, 150) points out, Kant had already explicitly rejected such a calculus by Maupertuis as early as 1763 at *NM*, 2:181.

IIb. Here the proposed theodicy is trying to show that physical ill is unavoidable. It is the opposite of that in IIa, namely that there is net physical ill. It states that "the preponderance of painful feelings over pleasant ones cannot be separated from the nature of an animal creature such as the human being" (*Failure*, 8:260). Busche's restates the three objections above to IIa but additionally he holds that Kant is making a personal judgment and not a normative one. In my view, Kant does not directly answer the challenge implied in the theodicy when he responds "then another question arises, namely why the creator of our existence called us into life when the latter, in our correct estimate is not desirable to us." This amounts to another acknowledgment of not knowing God's ways which was highlighted in the first group of theodicies. Also called into question but left open here is why a good God would make his creation suffer. It is likely that here Kant again had Leibniz's *Theodicy* in mind as the latter also uses the tale of Genghis Khan and an Indian woman at §177/H237 when examining this proposed theodicy. It would otherwise be a most remarkable coincidence that both use the same device.

IIc. In effect, this theodicy sets out to answer the question remaining open from IIb. It runs:

> God has put us here on earth for the sake of a future happiness . . . yet an arduous and sorrowful state in the present life must without exception precede that hoped-for superabundant blessedness—a state in which we are to become worthy of that future glory precisely through our struggle with adversities. (*Failure*, 8:260)

This is clearly a "higher purpose" or "greater good" theodicy and one to which Kant does not have a rebuttal which is not in the form of a further, deeper question. He admits that "in no way can there be insight into it." Moreover, this problem of no insight is an important theme to which Kant returns in dealing with all nine theodicies as a group. He ends his consideration, just as he did at *Opt*, 2:29, with a possible allusion to the Gordian Knot, a famous example of not accepting a problem as given but solving it in another manner. Kant acknowledges the attempted theodicy has failed to offer a meaningful explanation but "one can indeed cut the knot loose [as did Alexander the Great] through an appeal to the highest wisdom which willed it, but one cannot untie the knot, which is what theodicy claims to be capable of accomplishing" (ibid.).

In offering an intermediate balance for the attempted theodicies dealing with physical ill contrasted with God's goodness, although Kant's arguments are less than knock-downs, it could be argued that he has shown considerable forbearance in even considering these three arguments. He has, once more, declined to use two of the weapons in the armory which he built up, this time from his pre-Critical period. The first is that physical ill is not a punishment for moral evil. The second is that physical ill is not evil at all, but rather natural harm, namely the negative effects for human beings of the continuous and regular working of the laws of nature. Thus reason need not be reconciled with God's moral attributes for such a class of supposed evil. This is consistent with my conclusion above that Kant now only sees one evil, moral evil. In turn, this further supports my view that Kant is reviewing commonly advanced theodicies from his time. Also noteworthy is that the type of theodicy Kant is critiquing here is no longer that of first group, namely *a priori*; it is now experiential or *a posteriori*.

In the third and final group of theodicies, Kant considers the charges of injustice against the "world's judge," in modern terms, against God's failure to deliver distributive justice. Before examining these, it is worthwhile asking, in the light of the conclusion drawn above that Kant recognizes only moral evil, is injustice a separately identifiable evil? In my view, strictly speaking, it is not. Injustice arises with the perceived mismatch between moral behavior and physical well-being/harm both when the morally evil man prospers or avoids punishment or when the good man suffers as result of others' moral evil. Hence injustice does not introduce another form of evil; it concerns the relationship between the two previous categories of moral evil and physical ill/natural harm. Nevertheless, this does not stop theodicies being offered which claim to address it and these Kant evaluates. However, should any type I theodicy dealing with moral evil have succeeded there would be no need to consider injustice in the world since there would be no moral evil against which to set human weal or woe.

IIIa. This theodicy attempts to show that the apparent counter-purposiveness of injustice is not so. Kant sets it out as "[t]he pretension that the depraved go unpunished in the world is ungrounded, for by its very nature every crime already carries with it its due punishment, inasmuch as the inner reproach of conscience torments the depraved even more harshly than the Furies" (*Failure*, 8:261). Kant dismisses this, regarding it as based on a misunderstanding where the good man with his moral sensitivities projects into the evil man how he (the good man) would feel in the same circumstances. Kant goes further and says that the depraved man only "laughs at the scrupulousness of the honest who inwardly plague themselves with self-inflicted rebukes" (ibid.). What really concerns the wicked man is avoiding punishment and Kant considers that the occasional reproach that the wicked man might feel does not spring from conscience and, in any event, is vastly outweighed by the pleasure that evil brings him. Kant's position here is in direct opposition to that in his pre-Critical period and in the early-Critical *Lectures* where the self-punishment by the wicked was accepted and to that extent supported a possible theodicy.

IIIb. In this theodicy the lack of the correct relation between guilt and punishment in this world is acknowledged in stating that "one must often witness with indignation a life led with crying injustice and yet happy to the end" whilst admitting that this is not "something inherent in nature and deliberately promoted, hence not a moral dissonance" (*Failure*, 8:261). Here, to accord with Kant's categorization scheme, the theodicy should be concerned with the unavoidability of injustice in this world. However, the theodicy presented here does not do this. Rather we are presented with a theodicy of the "higher purpose" type similar to IIc with injustice now playing the instrumental role and providing the moral proving ground in place of physical evil. Kant describes the attempted theodicy as "it is a property of virtue that it should wrestle with adversities . . . and sufferings only serve to enhance the value of virtue; thus, the dissonance of undeserved ills resolves itself before reason into a glorious moral melody" (ibid.). Whilst accepting that such a moral melody might from time to time swell up when "at least the end of life crowns virtue and punishes the depraved," Kant's objection to the theodicy is grounded on the many cases where this does not happen. Further, "the suffering seems to have happened to the virtuous, not *so that* his virtue should be pure, but *because* it was pure . . . and this is the very opposite of justice" (*Failure*, 8:262). This reintroduces the notion of the Highest Good which Kant introduced in the first *Critique* and which he defined as virtue in compliance with the moral law and happiness in proper proportion to such compliance.[4] This Highest Good is clearly the opposite of injustice. In the second *Critique*, Kant postulated immortality based on the non-achievability of the Highest Good in this life but, surprisingly, in closing his consideration, he casts doubt on both immortality and moral faith:

> For as regards the possibility that the end of this terrestrial life might not perhaps be the end of all life, such a possibility cannot count as *vindication* of providence; rather, it is merely a decree of morally believing reason which directs the doubter to patience but does not satisfy him. (Ibid.)

A potential resolution of this seeming inconsistency is that here Kant is dealing with philosophical theodicies which concern knowledge based on theoretical or speculative reason whereas in the second *Critique* he is concerned with what can be the subject of faith based on practical reason.

IIIc. This theodicy again acknowledges injustice in the "disharmonious relation between the moral worth of human beings and the lot which befalls them" but our attention is directed toward "the use of the human faculties according to the laws of nature, in proportion to the skill and the prudence of their application" (ibid.). In other words, human beings are the source of the injustice to be found in this world and we should not measure such injustice by comparison with "supersensible ends." This is contrasted with a future world where "a different order of things will obtain" and again this is an indirect reference to the Highest Good mentioned in connection with IIIb but, again surprisingly, Kant finds such an assumption "arbitrary." This time, however, he does provide the reasoning behind this stance. Whilst the Highest Good can be a product of practical, moral, reason, again theoretical reason is limited by what can be gained from experience. Thus we have no mandate under *theoretical* reason for any argument other than in a future world where the same disharmonious relationship between moral worth and deserts will obtain.

> [T]here is no comprehensible relation between the inner grounds of determination of the will (namely the moral way of thinking) according to the laws of freedom, and the (for the most part external) causes of our welfare independent of our will according to the laws of nature, so the presumption remains that the

agreement of human fate with a divine justice . . . is just as little to be expected there as here. (*Failure*, 8:262)

This passage reprises not only the contrast between intelligible freedom and sensible determination established in the first *Critique* but also, in the final part, the limitations of theoretical, speculative, reason. Using this, we can only project that the mismatch between virtue and well-being which we experience in this world will also apply in the next. If this theodicy were to succeed, Kant's stance on the Highest Good would thus be undermined. Finally, with this response to theodicy IIIc, Kant has prepared the way for his own theodicy grounded on practical, moral reasoning.

SUMMARY OF THEODICY EVALUATION

The results of Kant's considerations can be usefully summarized in the matrix form introduced earlier.

Table 7.2   Summary of Evaluation

	I. Moral Evil vs. Holiness	*II. Physical Ill vs. Goodness*	*III. Injustice vs. Justice*
a. Denial of Evil	God has own standard of morality but this would make God evil, which Kant rejects.	There is more good than evil in the world. Dismissed as "sophistry."	The evil person suffers through guilt, injustice is denied. Firmly rejected. The evil man does not suffer guilt; only the good man.
b. Evil Unavoidable	God could not avoid making a world with evil thus intentional evil is denied. Theodicy rejected as it would deny moral evil.	There is more evil than good in the world. Physical evil is unavoidable but a good God would not have made people suffer. God's ways unknown.	Suffering increases moral worth but it seems that the virtuous suffer on account of their virtue. An unsatisfactory outcome.
c. Evil Human Fault, Not that of God	A special case of Ib. Again God not responsible for evil. He has permitted it for higher purposes. Kant sees man not responsible. for limitations inherent in creation.	Suffering leads to future happiness. Rejected as just responding to one theodicy with another.	There will be a final balance between goodness and reward but no proof of this from sensible world using theoretical reason.

In addition to summarizing the results at an individual theodicy level, it is appropriate to also assess Kant's overall argumentation and the success, or otherwise, of the legal analogy which he set up. In my view, given the way he structured his analysis, Kant's arguments, varying from outright dismissal to detailed rebuttal, are patchy, including some counter-assertions which Busche holds are just Kant's personal views. In other cases, his arguments do not address the specific contrast, readily derived from the matrix, which he has set up between theodicy type and divine attribute. So my conclusion here is that Kant has not made a good case against the attempted theodicy in all nine cases. This conclusion is broadly in line with that of Busche but he goes further and concludes that Kant's overall effort to dismiss the nine theodicies has failed– –*das Mißlingen ist mißlungen*. He also criticizes the application of the legal analogy with Kant often treating theodicy's defender as the accused rather than God and Kant himself being variously both prosecutor and judge. However, it is at the following step where Busche and I differ. I contend that the quality of Kant's argument in response to these theodicies and any shortcomings in these nine cases do not matter since Kant has solid grounds to dismiss philosophical theodicies *as a class*. In this too, I differ from Busche who considers Kant's arguments in favor of such a dismissal are also defective (cf. 2012, 267).

Kant does not provide any statement whether the nine attempted theodicies exhaust all possibilities or are merely examples of the then prevailing theodicies. I incline toward the latter option with his scheme providing a way of systematizing those theodicies known to him, some of which are still commonplace even today with people rationalizing illness or untimely death with "it was God's way" or accepting setbacks with threadbare platitudes such as "to get their reward the good must suffer in this life." However, I believe that providing a definitive answer to this question is unimportant as again, if Kant is dismissing philosophical theodicies as a class, it does not matter whether or not he has considered all the individual theodicies which exhaust that class. I also hold that whether the individual dismissals of the nine theodicies succeed or fail is irrelevant since Kant is dismissing them because of their common property of invalidly claiming insight into God's ways of working based on our experience of the world. Kant makes his move to this conclusion when confirming:

> Every previous theodicy has not performed what it promised, namely the vindication of the moral wisdom of the world-government against the doubts raised against it on the basis of what the experience of the world teaches. (*Failure*, 8:263)

However, he goes on to say that, if God has failed to be acquitted before the tribunal of reason, equally He has failed to be convicted of the alleged offences against His holiness, goodness, and justice, an agnostic result.

However that will not do as it is Kant's aim to bring the trial to an end "once and for all" but he recognizes that this will not be possible until it can be firmly established that "our reason is absolutely incapable of insight into *the relationship in which any world as we may ever become acquainted with through experience stands with respect to the highest wisdom*" (ibid.). This would require knowledge of God but in the first *Critique* Kant has shown that this impossible for us in the world of experience. However, Kant considers that such a result at least demonstrates a "negative wisdom . . . namely the insight into the necessary limitation of what we may presume with respect to that which is too high for us" (ibid.). However, and surprisingly, Kant does not fully exploit this argument but develops another one. This could be taken to mean that he regards the argument from the first *Critique* as insufficient but I discount this as such an interpretation would seriously undermine the imposing metaphysical and epistemological edifice which Kant erected in that work. The alternative, which I favor, is that Kant wants to provide some case specific justification to supplement the general argument from the first *Critique*. From our experience of the world we have a concept of the artistic wisdom of God which underpins the physico-theology to which Kant remained attracted throughout his career. To this Kant adds that:

> [W]e also have in the moral idea of our own practical reason a concept of moral wisdom which could have been implanted in the world in general by a most perfect creator.—But of the unity of agreement in a sensible world between that artistic and moral wisdom we have no concept; nor can we ever hope to attain one. (Ibid.)

This short passage contains two important elements. First, again, Kant is confirming the role of practical reason in giving some indication of God's moral purposes. Second, we are incapable of the synthetic combination of God's artistic wisdom, derived from the apparent purposiveness of the world which we experience, and His moral wisdom.[5] Schulte provides a concise summary of this impossibility:

> Theodicy fails generally because it is impossible for the defender of theodicy to bridge the gulf between the intelligible world of divine teleology [wisdom] and the bad state of affairs in the empirical world by means of finite reason (1991, 391; author's translation)

This inability to bridge this gulf is a recurring challenge but one which should not surprise us as the separation between the sensible and the intelligible, phenomenal and noumenal, is fundamental to Kant's metaphysics. Also recalling his differentiation between *Böse* and *Übel*, this is not a German word-game; *Böse* inhabits the intelligible world, the world of freedom; *Übel* inhabits the sensible world, the world of nature. The inability to bridge these worlds lies at not only at the heart of the failure of philosophical theodicies but also of injustice, the opposite of the Highest Good.

This is the reason why any attempt to address any shortcomings in the arguments of the nine theodicies is nugatory. Moreover, this is also why the questions whether the nine are an exhaustive list and whether his dismissals of the individual theodicies are watertight do not require answers. Any theodicy reliant on theoretical reason yielding knowledge of God would also fail. This may seem a negative result, but it is important that in this way, Kant clears the field of *all* philosophical theodicies before advancing a theodicy of his own. In supporting Kant's argument that all philosophical theodicies can be dismissed as a class because of our inability to combine God's artistic wisdom with His moral wisdom, I am also taking a position contra Duncan. In contrast, Duncan (cf. 2012, 981–82) holds that he gave up on theodicies *prior* to *Failure* because, realizing from the work of C. C. E. Schmid that creaturely limitation led to evil necessarily which absolves man from liability for moral evil. No, Kant wanted an account based on the moral responsibility which stems from man's freedom to act.

Despite my agreement with Kant's dismissal of philosophical theodicies on principle, there are still well-founded overall concerns about the exercise which he undertook. The first potential problem concerns the "tribunal of reason" which Kant set up. He is clear on the role that the tribunal of reason plays in the evaluation of theodicies (cf. *Failure*, 8:255). However, Kant's conclusion concerning "the outcome of this juridical process before the forum of philosophy" (*Failure*, 8:263) is that the attempted vindications of God's moral wisdom have not only failed but failed structurally because of their impossibility of ever doing so. Kant is not being inconsistent in this matter. He has insisted that reason is used to examine potential theodicies but, by proceeding in this way, Kant has again demonstrated the limitations of the speculative, theoretical, reason being employed. Thus it is possible to regard his examination of the nine attempted theodicies as an extended heuristic device which clears the path for his argument for a non-philosophical theodicy using practical reason, recalling the special sense in which Kant is using "philosophical" in this context, namely to denote theodicies based on theoretical, speculative reason.

The second potential problem concerns knowledge of God's properties. In the first *Critique*, Kant demonstrates that whilst we can have an idea of God (being an Ideal of Pure Reason), we cannot have any knowledge of Him. In the second *Critique*, God is a postulate of practical reason. In *Failure* (8:257) God's properties are identified as (i) holiness as author of the world (law-giver), (ii) goodness as ruler, and (iii) justice as judge. Kant offers us no derivation of these properties beyond stating that these are "[t]he attributes of the world-author's supreme wisdom." This repeats an earlier claim for the same three attributes made in *Lectures* (cf. 28:1073). Kant holds that if we think about a being without any of these three attributes, we are not thinking about the moral God but something else. Yet there is an apparent discrepancy here in that we are denied knowledge of God but we can rationally postulate that he has the three listed moral properties. In my view, a resolution is possible as Kant shows that God's moral properties do not come from the speculative use of pure reason but rather from the demands of practical reason with the latter overriding the former as stated in the second *Critique* (cf. *CPR*, 5:119–21). This is the answer to the problem of the unresolved ontological status of God discussed in the previous chapter, namely God is constitutive entity for the purposes of practical moral reason. This is a view endorsed by Byrne when, despite his predominantly anti-realist stance on God, he suggests that the attributes under discussion here are characterized by their utility:

> The predicates we use to fill out the picture we have of God do not function to pick out attributes which God might actually have. Instead, they fill out the picture we must have of God if our practical purposes are to be served. (2007, 67–68)

In sum, Kant's conclusion that philosophical theodicies fail is sound despite any objections which can be brought against his arguments in rejecting the individual theodicies which he considered. Our way is now clear to revisit his taxonomy of evil as a prerequisite to our examination of Kant's own "authentic" theodicy. This step is needed since, just as was done in considering Kant's pre-Critical period, if the examination of authentic theodicy is to yield a definite result, certainty is needed concerning what Kant saw evil as encompassing.

NOTES

1. As long as Leibniz's theodicy is held to have an *a priori* basis, it is exempt from this stricture.
2. The numbering system used for the triads having been chosen to align with Kant's theodicy categorisation used in *Failure*, 8:258–62. Professor Stephen Palmquist (2000, 456) is acknowledged as the originator of the matrix method of presentation used here.
3. This view was previously advanced by Leibniz (H379) in the Second Objection of the Summary of the Controversy Reduced to Formal Arguments.
4. Further consideration of the Highest Good is held over to a later chapter of this study.
5. God's moral wisdom will be considered again in chapter 9.

Chapter 8

The Taxonomy of Evil Revisited

INTRODUCTORY REMARKS

Yakira writes that "Kant does not cease returning to the philosophical question of the religion. However, this interest for the religion is always related to the question of evil" (2009, 153). This is a good reason to now do the same. In the previous chapter, I maintained that with *Failure,* in his consideration of theodicy Ic (cf. *Failure,* 8:259), Kant recognized that creatures' necessary limitations were not evil for which they were morally responsible, but merely the condition of possibility of such evil. However, in Part II of this study dealing with Kant's early-Critical period, a significant unresolved tension was noted from the presence in *Lectures* of the following: "[e]vil has *no special germ; for it is mere negation* and consists only in the *limitation of the good.* It is nothing beyond this" (*Lect,* 28:1078). This is seemingly in direct opposition to Kant's stance on metaphysical evil conceived as limitation in *Failure.* Not only is moral evil apparently excluded here but Kant appears to be going one step further and saying that the limitation itself is evil and not that the limitation is just the ground of possibility for evil. This passage from *Lectures* also conflicts with the argument which I developed in the pre-Critical part of this study (Part I). This was that, in *Negative Magnitudes* of 1763, in addition to recognizing evil as a limitation, Kant saw evil as ontologically positive but with a negative value when compared to the good. One possible response could be to claim that Kant simply changed his mind by the time he gave the *Lectures* in 1783/1784 and then changed it back again in 1791. But that would be weak with a lack of supporting evidence for such a flip-flop. Another possible response could be to abandon my *Negative Magnitudes* argument that a fundamental change had taken place in Kant's thinking. Should this line be taken, it would at least allow a claim to be made for continuity, namely that in *Lectures* Kant was just maintaining the essentially Leibnizian position he initially adopted in his pre-Critical period. However, I will not be taking that course as I consider my argument from *Negative Magnitudes* to be sound and fully supported by those advanced by Schönfeld[1] and Heimsoeth[2] on the topic. Moreover in *Religion,* Kant provides further evidence for my argument by unambiguously restating the key claim of *Negative Magnitudes* in theory at 6:22n and then applying it to evil in the following manner:

> Now, if the law fails nevertheless to determine somebody's free power of choice with respect to an action relating to it, an incentive *opposed to it* must have influence on the power of choice of the human being in question. (*Rel*, 6:24; emphasis added)

Finally, abandoning my *Negative Magnitudes* argument would do nothing to address the later contrast between *Lectures* and *Failure*.

Nonetheless, these apparent inconsistencies demand a re-examination of Kant's taxonomy of evil to determine whether a unified account can be produced. If not, this issue has the potential to undermine Kant's case for his own, authentic, theodicy. Are the two positions, evil as ontologically positive and evil as a limitation, indeed in any kind of competition? If they are not, neither need be abandoned. This re-examination requires a step back in time to look briefly again at Leibniz's taxonomy of evil. Then a temporary jump forward is needed, past our current concern with *Failure* to *Religion* as this work contains Kant's definitive stance on the source and nature of evil. I will argue that metaphysical evil conceived as limitation and Kant's concept of radical evil introduced in *Religion* perform the same function and further, neither is in conflict with the idea of ontologically real moral evil, a permanent element in Kant's taxonomy from 1763 onwards.

EVIL: LEIBNIZ AND KANT IN *FAILURE* COMPARED

For Leibniz there were three classes of evil: metaphysical, physical, and moral. In *Failure*, Kant also considered three types of evil: moral, physical, and injustice. But I have argued that, for him, only moral evil needs to be addressed. He calls it "evil proper (sin)" (*Failure*, 8:256). A taxonomy of just a single evil is supported by Emile Fackenheim who writes "by evil we do not mean pain, disease, death, etc. No doubt these abound but we are not concerned with them. Our concern is solely with moral evil" (1996, 27) and calling on Kant in support citing "nothing is morally evil [i.e., capable of being imputed] but that which is our own *act*" (*Rel*, 6:31). Indeed, support for this interpretation can be found within Kant's writings when he is discussing the propensity to evil in *Religion* where he states that "we are only talking of a propensity to *genuine* evil, i.e., moral evil" (*Rel*, 6:29; emphasis added). In other words, the only evil which is real for the late-Critical Kant is moral evil. As previously stated, it is only in order to evaluate then-current theodicies, that Kant considers physical ill and its possible relationship to moral evil. I hold that Kant's substantive position remained that which he developed in his pre-Critical period, namely that physical ill is not punishment for moral evil but is rather natural harm[3] where this is the injury done to humans as a result of the unchanging, continuous, and ubiquitous laws of nature.

However, Kant considers a third category namely injustice—the "disproportion between crimes and penalties in the world" (*Failure*, 8:257). But this, I have argued earlier, does not introduce a new type of evil but rather deals with the particular relationship between virtue/moral evil and un/happiness. Significantly, there is no mention of metaphysical evil in *Failure*. Kant's taxonomy is complete without it. Indeed, Busche goes so far as to compliment Kant for having excluded metaphysical evil from his taxonomy stating "nevertheless Kant does well to not once introduce a metaphysically counter-purposive[4] as a fourth ground of complaint [against God]" (2013, 245).[5] I shall briefly return to the question of this exclusion. Notwithstanding, in *Religion*, the publication of which immediately followed *Failure*, Kant introduced radical evil which was not included in the taxonomy of *Failure*. This I will argue is the potential to do evil and not evil *per se*. In that case, it is not an additional evil which Kant wrongly excluded from consideration in *Failure*.

METAPHYSICAL EVIL FOR LEIBNIZ

Should God, as infinite and the most real, create something which is also infinite and most real, then it would be another God which is impossible. Therefore, when God creates, He must create something which is both less real and finite; indeed the concept of a creature *per se* includes being limited. The result is that creatures do not and cannot contain the complete good which is only found in God. This shortfall in goodness Leibniz regards as metaphysical evil. However, for Leibniz, metaphysical evil is also the ultimate condition of possibility of all evil, moral evil thus included. This can be seen from his statements that "considering the metaphysical good and evil which is in all substances, whether endowed with or devoid of intelligence, and which taken so broadly would include physical good and moral good" (§263/H288) and "the metaphysical good which includes everything makes it necessary sometimes to admit physical evil and moral evil" (§209/H258). Leibniz is clear in the Preface to the *Theodicy* at H57 that "the freedom of the will, so essential to the morality of action: for justice and injustice, praise and blame . . . cannot attach to necessary[6] actions" and in *Theodicy* proper that "freedom is deemed necessary,[7] in order that man may be deemed guilty and open to punishment" (§1/H123).[8] Now at §20/H135 Leibniz states that "we must consider that there is an original imperfection in the creature because the creature is limited in its essence." From these elements the following argument can be distilled:

1. What is necessary (could not be otherwise) is unfree (H57).
2. A creature *qua* creature is essentially (necessarily) limited (§20/H135).
3. To the extent that a creature is limited, it is unfree (from 1, 2).
4. Freedom is required for moral accountability (§1/H123).
5. Evil arising from limitation is not morally accountable (from 3, 4).

The original imperfection (metaphysical evil arising from limitation), as it is part of man's essence (cf. §20/H135), must be antecedent to any evil for which man is accountable. The latter is moral evil which requires the condition of freedom to be accountable. This means that metaphysical evil conceived as limitation on its own is insufficient for moral evil. This is supported by Antognazza in the following and with which I concur:

> It seems . . . that metaphysical evil, intended as this original limitation, has strictly the character of *malum in se*. That is, ontologically, it is strictly non-being. In other words, although creaturely limitation is formally evil (*malum in se*) insofar as it qualifies as an instance of non-being, it does not on its own make a creature to some degree or in some respect evil. (2014, 133)

From these considerations I contend that it is justified to regard metaphysical evil from limitation not as "real," that is ontologically positive, but rather it is the condition of possibility to commit moral evil, a stance also adopted by Brachtendorf (2002, 72). It is not the active *malum culpae* with the perpetrator, in Leibniz's taxonomy, deserving of physical evil as *malum poenae*. In other words, it is the condition of the possibility of our doing wrong but it is still inexpugnably part of being human, a creature capable of (im)moral actions.

KANT'S RADICAL EVIL

It is useful to clear up first one possible misconception concerning radical evil, namely that it is Kant's term for horrendous evil. This is an understandable natural reading where "radical" is taken to mean "extreme." No, it is rather the mechanism by which Kant explains the presence of evil in mankind. By examining the etymology of the word "radical" James DiCenso (2012, 38) offers a helpful description, "it [radical evil] rather indicates the root (*radix*) of evil within our inherent freedom to choose."[9] This also suggests that radical evil is the ground for evil not the evil which is done and, in my view, there is ample evidence in *Religion* to support such an interpretation, an example being Kant's description: "[t]his evil is radical, since it corrupts the ground of all maxims" (*Rel*, 6:37). In other words, it undermines the subjective grounds of our actions, but it does not constitute the actions themselves. Even more explicitly, Kant states that it is "the *formal* ground of every deed contrary to law" (*Rel*, 6:32; emphasis added) and thus not the deed itself.

Kant is concerned to show in *Religion*, just as in the *Groundwork*, that moral responsibility rests on the individual through the exercise of freedom in selecting maxims which either comply with or contravene the moral law. He is keen to ensure that when we say that someone is good or bad by nature, it does not mean that that person is necessitated to act in a good or bad way but rather "that he holds within himself a first ground (to us inscrutable) for the adoption of good or evil (unlawful) maxims" (*Rel*, 6:21). Further, this ground, the individual's deep-seated *Gesinnung*, is a matter of choice which Kant describes as follows:

> The disposition, i.e., the first subjective ground of the adoption of the maxims, can only be a single one, and it applies to the entire use of freedom universally. This disposition too, however, must be adopted through the free power of choice, for otherwise it could not be imputed. (*Rel*, 6:25)

However, Kant holds that we cannot go looking for the maxim for this first subjective ground as it would have its ground in turn and so on, leading to an infinite regress. In my view, it is for this reason that Kant terms this choice noumenal to free it from such infinite regress. This noumenal moral agency, the capacity to fundamentally choose evil, is something we have *qua* human and it is for this reason Kant wants to term it innate. Kant confirms this when he terms evil "innate only in this sense, that it is posited as the ground antecedent to every use of freedom in experience[10] (in earliest youth as far back as our birth) and is thus conceived of as present in man at birth" (*Rel*, 6:22). This establishes Kant's view that this propensity as the ground necessary for evil but not the evil itself. At several places in *Religion* Kant stresses that this attribute is from our limitations as a species, not as individual agents. For example, "if it is legitimate to assume that this propensity belongs to the human being universally (and hence to the character of the species), this propensity will be called a *natural* propensity of the human being to evil"

(*Rel*, 6:29). It arises from our createdness, our finitude. Moreover, in the *Groundwork* at *GW*, 4:405, Kant had previously talked about such a propensity which seemed to be endemic to the human condition. Importantly, it is not the good or evil which is innate but rather the power of choice for good or evil. Although he does not explicitly position two additional key notions which are advanced in *Religion* under the power of choice, Kant underpins the effect of choice by asserting that we have both a predisposition to the good and a propensity to evil.[11] He states that "I represent the relationship of the good and the evil principles as two equally self-subsisting transient causes affecting men" (*Rel*, 6:11). It cannot be an either/or situation since if an individual had only one that person would be permanently good or evil and thus incapable of change which is far removed from Kant's position. It is this propensity to evil which Kant calls radical evil as it is this which lies at the root of all our evil actions (cf. *Rel*, 6:32). It should be again emphasized, however, that the propensity to evil is not the evil which is done. This becomes even clearer when Kant describes this propensity as "*peccatum in potentia*" (*Rel*, 6:40).

It is also useful here to recall Kant's view on the uniqueness of human beings which is that we have two natures, a sensible, animal nature (affected by and affecting the phenomenal world) and an intelligible rational nature (capable of formulating and willing according to reason and moral principles).[12] Beings that are solely animal in nature do no wrong because they do not have the means to differentiate between good and bad acts. Indeed, we regard human beings who through accidents of birth do not reach a certain threshold level of rationality as not morally responsible for their actions. At the other end of the spectrum beings with only a fully rational nature, such as angels would have, should they exist, could only do right actions and hence they would not display virtue since they cannot *choose* to follow the moral law. This is a position which Kant clearly confirms in the *Metaphysics of Morals*, stating that "for finite holy beings there would be no doctrine of virtue but only a doctrine of morals" (*MM*, 6:383). In the *Groundwork* Kant shows *a priori* that, arising from our rationality, we become aware of the moral law within us. However, from our sensible nature we have inclinations which when taken up into maxims, the subjective grounds for our actions, either comply with or contravene that moral law. When we choose to act on maxims of the former type, we do good; when we choose the latter type, often the most powerful ones relying on self-interest[13] or inertia, we do evil. Again, it is a matter of choice under the conditions of freedom. It is because we can do otherwise that we have, uniquely, the duty or obligation to obey the moral law. From this it can be seen that if we had only a predisposition to the good, we would be incapable of moral or immoral actions. Equally, should only a propensity to evil be present we would only do evil and the escape from evil which Kant in *Religion* bases on a revolutionary change of heart, or becoming a new man, (cf. *Rel*, 6:47), would be impossible. Kant ascribes our ability to effect this change of heart to the presupposition "that there is still a germ of goodness left in its entire purity, a germ which cannot be extirpated or corrupted" (*Rel*, 6:45). Thus both the propensity to evil and predisposition to the good are permanently present in man and compete with each other for ascendency.

RESOLVING THE COMPETING ACCOUNTS OF EVIL

Kant states that "Evil can have originated only from moral evil (not just from the limitations of our nature)" (*Rel*, 6:43). There are two ways of reading this. First, that evil can only have come from moral evil and no other source or, second, that evil came from moral evil *in combination* with the limitations *qua* human.[14] Moreover, for Kant to suggest that limitations are the ground of evil in the same work, *Religion*, in which he advances the notion of radical evil, must mean that he cannot have seen them as conflicting if he is to be regarded as having produced a consistent account. When one takes the second reading above, which in my view is the correct one, a resolution of the difficulty with which we started emerges. This would mean that (i) the ontologically positive evil of 1763 in *Negative Magnitudes* and (ii) the metaphysical evil arising from limitation endorsed by Kant in his pre-Critical period and apparently restated by him in 1783/1784 in *Lectures* are not mutually exclusive. On the contrary, I contend that these notions are mutually supportive.

In the discussion above we have seen that the metaphysical evil from limitation is not ontologically positive but rather a potential to do evil due to human finitude and which cannot be altered. We have seen too that radical evil is a potential to do evil which is again a human characteristic which, in Kant's terms, cannot be extirpated but only overcome through an ongoing resolve to obey the moral law (cf. *Rel*, 6:37). So the first reconciliation offered is that metaphysical evil conceived as limitation and radical evil perform the same function, namely providing the ultimate ground for the possibility of evil in the world. They have been developed from very different starting points but share a common end point of being inherent in human createdness. This reconciliation is consistent with Kant's later statement in *Lectures* that "if we ask where the evil in individual human beings comes from, the answer is that it exists on account of the limits necessary to every creature" (*Lect*, 28:1079). To my mind, the natural reading of this is that Kant is advancing the ground of evil not describing an evil *per se*. The proposed reconciliation would also fully answer the question that Duncan (2012, 988) poses: "it is not clear whether the *Religion*'s theory of evil develops and makes explicit what is implicit and undeveloped in Kant's previous works or if it indicates a shift in Kant's views." I consider the former to be correct.

But what sort of evil? It is the moral evil named by both by Leibniz in *Theodicy* and by Kant in *Failure*. Further, given Kant's stance on physical evil as natural harm, it can *only* be moral evil which Kant was referring to when he argued in *Negative Magnitudes* for a positive ontology of evil. Moreover, arguing that evil is ontologically positive is not incompatible with its ground (as the condition of its possibility) being sought elsewhere. This means that the pre-Critical Kant was not setting two types of evil in opposition but rather elucidating two different things, namely the *nature* of evil as experienced in the world (as ontologically positive) with its *ground* (limitation). Continuing to see a conflict between them is to be mistaken. This is what I take Duncan to be doing in his 2012 paper where he contends that Kant made a late career switch from evil as limitation to ontologically positive evil in order not to assign responsibility for evil to God. Moreover, the resolution advanced here does not impact Kant's taxonomy of evil in the immediately preceding work, *Failure*, since in that work Kant is concerned with evil as commonly reported, not with its ground. In this way, Busche's compliment to Kant for omitting metaphysical evil from *Failure* is well made. So, in sum, the tensions between the various accounts of evil can be disarmed with the two reconciliations which have been put forward. These are: first, that Kant's radical evil, his propensity to evil, performs the same function as Leibniz's metaphysical evil conceived as limitation; second, that Leibniz's moral evil in *Theodicy* is Kant's ontologically positive evil in *Negative Magnitudes* and the moral evil in *Failure*.

In conclusion, it should be stressed that Kant himself neither argued for any such account nor sought any reconciliation of the apparent difficulty reported in *Lectures* which prompted this re-examination of evil. What is being advanced here is not to be found explicitly in any of Kant's writings; it is a hidden harmony. If the proposed account is accepted, the challenge with which we started is solved and we are no longer seeking to explain conflicts between the *Negative Magnitudes* of 1763, the *Lectures* of twenty years later and *Failure* in 1791; these works are simply dealing with different aspects of evil. This has not been an irrelevant academic diversion without any bearing on the purposes of this study. It removes the final possible threat to Kant's position that evil results from our freedom and therefore we bear responsibility for moral evil. This unified account of evil can now underpin the further consideration of Kant on theodicy *per se* to which we can now return with renewed confidence.

NOTES

1. Cf. Schönfeld (2000, 188).
2. Cf. Heimsoeth (1966, 227).
3. Once more this is a part of Leibnizian metaphysical evil under Antognazza's classification (cf. 2014, 122ff.).
4. In *Failure*, "counter-purposive" is Kant's overarching description of all types of evil.
5. Author's translation.
6. To my reading "necessary" is being used here in the sense of "could not be otherwise."
7. To my reading "necessary" is being used here in the sense of "required."
8. Kant's stance on the necessity of freedom for moral accountability is no different.
9. See also Allison (1990, 147) in support of these definitional points.
10. It is extra-experience which makes it noumenal.
11. For the purposes of this study a full exposition of these two characteristics is not needed but a full account is to be found at *Rel*, 6:26–32.
12. The two descriptions in parentheses are taken from DiCenso (2012).
13. Or self-love, in Kant's terms.
14. Duncan (2012, 987) goes one step further to claim that "Kant explicitly says that evil cannot spring from our limitations" but I do not support such an interpretation.

Chapter 9

Kant's Own Authentic Theodicy

CONSTRAINTS ON POSSIBLE THEODICY

Although Kant did not put forward an explicit theodicy of his own in his early-Critical period, the constraints on any theodicy should he have done so were listed earlier. It is useful, before examining his own theodicy, to update this list to reflect the changes in Kant's thought on theodicy by 1791. Kant had to remain within these constraints to be consistent. It is important, however, to keep in mind that these constraints have not been imposed on him from any outside source, whether philosophical or theological; they are solely the result of his considerations to date. They are:

1. Philosophical theodicies based on the arguments of theoretical/speculative reason drawn from our experience of the world do not and cannot succeed.
2. Theodicies based on a claimed knowledge of God are ruled out by the epistemology of the first *Critique*. This acts to debar all attempted philosophical theodicies, past, present, and future.
3. Also invalidated are theodicies which call on any of the three traditional proofs of God's existence which Kant dismissed.
4. Kant regards that which had been traditionally termed physical evil not as evil at all; it is the workings of the ubiquitous and unchanging laws of nature with disadvantageous outcomes for human beings. Theodicy does not have to account for such natural harm as it has been termed in this study.
5. Attempted free-will theodicies grounded on God's wanting something from us other than compliance with the moral law are rejected.
6. The challenge of injustice in the world remains but it concerns the relationship between moral evil/virtue and natural harm/well-being. It is not a separate category of evil.

7. The metaphysical evil arising from the unavoidable limitation in finite created beings no longer has to be accounted in a theodicy since it is the ground of the possibility of evil, not the evil itself. Only moral evil remains to be accounted for. It is real; that is it is ontologically positive.[1]

These constraints limit Kant's freedom of maneuver and it should not be a surprise when Kant gives us an indication of this in a concise yet powerful footnote early in *Failure* that it is the moral route to a theodicy which he will follow:

> [T]he concept of God suited to religion must be a concept of him as moral being (for we have no need of him for natural explanation) . . . and since this concept can just as little be derived from the mere transcendental concept of an absolutely necessary being . . . as be founded on experience; so it is clear enough that the proof of the existence of such a being can be none other than a moral proof. (*Failure*, 8:256n)[2]

In one of the most frequently quoted passages from Kant's works he says in the Preface to the second edition of the first *Critique* "thus I had to deny *knowledge* in order to make room for *faith*" (Bxxx, emphasis in original). This suggests that where Kant now finds himself was his deliberate destination and not that he had painted himself into a theodical corner.

AUTHENTIC THEODICY

In putting forward his authentic theodicy, Kant does not make the task easy for those who wish to understand or reconstruct his argument, giving us a merely a half page in *Failure* which is difficult even by Kant's own standards and is seemingly inconsistent in places. He follows this with an example of authentic theodicy which helps in understanding his stance, before enlarging on the key subject of sincerity in the Concluding Remark. However, after tracing his thinking through these various stages, it will be seen, despite the initial difficulties, that there can be no doubt that Kant's own theodicy is one based on moral faith resting on the moral proof attested to in the citation above from *Failure*, 8:256n.

Kant opens his argument by stating that "[a]ll theodicy should truly be an interpretation of nature insofar as God announces his will through it" (*Failure*, 8:264). This is surprising since was this not what Kant was addressing in the nine attempted theodicies? Showing why they necessarily fail, namely to derive God's purpose from our experience in the world? An "interpretation of nature" seems to be just that. As often with Kant when he appears to contradict himself, as he seems to do at this point, it is a reasonable (and charitable) hypothesis to assume, if only temporarily, that he meant something other than the natural reading. I believe this to be the case here. Kant continues by stating that any theodicy is either *doctrinal* or *authentic*. His description of the former as "a rational inference of that will from the utterances of which the law-giver has made use" (ibid.) sheds very little light on the differentiation which he is introducing. Further, the natural reading of "doctrinal" suggests something based on a text claimed as revealed or on church teachings, but this is not Kant's intent. Supporting this reading is that this is not Kant's first use of "doctrinal" in the sense used here. Rather, it is consistent with his use of the term in the first *Critique* where he states "there is in merely theoretical judgments an *analogue* of practical judgments, where taking them to be true is aptly described by the word *belief*, and which we can call *doctrinal beliefs*" (A825/B853, emphasis in original).

In other words, theoretical judgments result in doctrinal beliefs. Unhelpfully, Kant does not give a clear-cut example of a law-giver's utterance of the type meant but provides an indirect clue to his thinking which also confirms the sense in which he is using "doctrinal":

> [T]he world ... is *often* a closed book for us, and it is so *every time* we look at it to extract from it God's *final aim* (which is always moral) even though it is an object of experience. Philosophical trials in this kind of interpretation are doctrinal. (*Failure*, 8:264)

This provides more solid ground as it was exactly the attempt to extract God's moral aim from our experience of the world which failed in the nine philosophical theodicies which Kant considered and rejected. Further, since in Kant's view, they failed necessarily rather than contingently, the conclusion can be drawn that he rejects all theodicies which he terms doctrinal.

However, just as progress is being made, Kant introduces another apparent inconsistency when discussing two types of potential theodicy:

> [i] Yet we cannot deny the name of "theodicy" also to the mere dismissal of all objections against divine wisdom, if this dismissal is a divine decree, or ...
> [ii] if it is a pronouncement of the same reason through which we form our concept of God—necessarily and prior to all experience—as a moral and wise being. (Ibid.)

The difficulty is with the first type. One of the conditions for the trial set up at the start of *Failure* was that simply dismissing objections against divine wisdom was not allowed but his statement seems to run counter to that. With the second theodicy type there is no problem since it is exactly what he will advance with "authentic" theodicy. He is saying that dismissal is allowed provided that it can be shown that it is based on the practical reason which yields our concept of God. So the "dismissal of all objections against divine wisdom" in the form of theodicy *is* allowed when based on moral grounds established by *a priori* practical reason. With this, Kant is making another significant move. He is expanding what is covered by the term "theodicy." Whereas previously theodicy was the province of theoretical/speculative reason it now embraces practical/moral reason too. Of course, Kant still has the challenge of providing such reasoning, but the distinction allows him to define authentic theodicy with "for through our [practical] reason God then becomes the interpreter of his will as announced through creation; and we can call this interpretation an *authentic* theodicy" (ibid.).

So an authentic theodicy must fulfill three criteria: (i) it is an utterance "made by the law-giver himself," (ii) it is given in creation, but (iii), above all it must be established by practical, moral reason. Because the moral law is grounded in reason it cannot be invalidated without denying our own rationality and since elsewhere he terms God the personification of the moral law, Kant is able to state that an authentic theodicy is "the unmediated definition and voice of God through which he gives meaning to the letter of his creation" (*Failure*, 8:264). "Voice," of course, is to be taken figuratively. Indeed, elsewhere Kant states that "[e]ven if God really spoke to man, the latter could never know that it was God who had been speaking" (*SF*, 7:63). This is because, per the first *Critique*, we have no knowledge of God. For Kant, the moral law is God's voice. We can also note a happy side-effect of Kant's terming his theodicy "authentic," the everyday meaning of which is "genuine." This is just what a theodicy based on practical/moral reason is for Kant.

It is certain that Kant regarded himself as advancing a theodicy here. Thus Duncan's choice of title for his 2012 paper "Moral Evil, Freedom and the Goodness of God: Why Kant abandoned Theodicy" is problematic, especially since Duncan does not consider Kant's authentic theodicy at all. But Duncan would have been correct if Kant had not expanded the meaning of "theodicy" in the way described above. However, what is paramount here is what *Kant* thought he was doing. I hold that Kant is not so much abandoning theodicy but giving it a new basis, a view supported by Brachtendorf (2002, 58).[3] It is now a *Glaubenssache*.[4] But we need also to identify the kind of faith involved. It is a faith grounded in morality which in turn is derived from our rationality. Thus it is an *a priori* rational faith not a fideistic one based on a supposedly revealed text. Brachtendorf summarizes Kant's argumentation well stating that he, Kant, has found a "middle way between a convinced rationalism and [at the other extreme] fideism which following the failure of rationalism wants to base theodicy on faith based on revelation rather than reason" (2002, 58; author's translation). Indeed, Kant had employed reason, now practical as opposed to theoretical, combined with a morally grounded faith in God in contrast to an ungrounded one as in fideism.

At this point, it would have been ideal if Kant had given us a concrete example of an authentic theodicy. However, what he gives us instead is his interpretation of the story of Job which he considers: "such an authentic interpretation expressed allegorically." Providing a full exposition of Job's story is not required, especially as Kant provides the succinct summary which is all that is needed:

> Job is portrayed as a man whose enjoyment of life included everything which anyone might possibly imagine it as making it complete. He was healthy, well-to-do ... surrounded by a happy family, among beloved friends—and ... (what is most important) at peace with himself in a good conscience. A harsh fate imposed in order to test him suddenly snatched from him all these blessings, except the last. (*Failure*, 8:265)

Nevertheless, there are rival interpretations of Job's woes. For his friends, Job's ills must stem from God's justice. Whilst they cannot identify any offences which Job has committed, they still hold that there is no such thing as innocent suffering. They are arguing *a priori* that any other interpretation would be "impossible according to divine justice." In other words, as summarized by Kenneth Seeskin (1987, 230), their case is "because God is undeniable, innocent suffering cannot occur." It can also be noted that in taking such a view, Job's friends are saying that there is a proportional relationship between happiness and virtue in *this* life, a situation describing an *immanent* Highest Good. In contrast, there is Job's own view where he says that he has done nothing wrong but accepts "the system of unconditional divine decision" (*Failure*, 8:265). Job remains conscious of God's presence in his life and does not rebel against Him. He acknowledges (his own) innocent suffering but this does not undermine his faith in God. Or in Seeskin's words, "What it shows is that Job does not think acknowledging innocent suffering is detrimental to belief in God" (1987, 231).

In arguing that God favors Job's view, Kant is being consistent with his rejection of speculative reason exceeding its bounds when claiming knowledge about God. Further, Job's story is demonstrating one consequence of the failure of all philosophical theodicies, namely that, for Kant, theodicy is now a matter of faith and not one of speculative, theoretical, reasoning. Kant has Job acknowledging this when he apologizes to God, stating:

> Since Job admits having hastily spoken about things which are too high for him and which he does not understand—not *as if wantonly*, for he is conscious of his honesty, but only unwisely. (*Failure*, 8:266)

The attractiveness of Job's attitude was not new for Kant in 1791 since in 1775 he had written to Lavater praising Job's attitude of not flattering God and for examining his innermost feelings (cf. 10:176). Job's stance is well described by Elizabeth Galbraith (2006, 184) "A refusal to give answers that do not match the facts characterizes Job's response to his own suffering." Such a refusal is, of course, what Kant has done in dismissing the nine attempted theodicies. Kant rejects the interpretation of Job's friends, because they are presuming that they know how God's justice works. In Seeskin's words, "the comforters [Job's friends] represent speculative reason's attempt to understand God on the basis of principles extrapolated from experience" (1987, 236) and which Kant rejected (cf. *Failure*, 8:263–64). Galbraith supports this interpretation stating that what Kant "seem[s] to have recognized in Job is an appropriate, for Kant fully vindicated, religious response to the inadequacy of traditional [philosophical] theodicies" (2006, 184).[5] A ringing endorsement of Job's stance comes when Kant states that "[f]or with this disposition he [Job] proved that he did not found his morality on faith, but his faith on morality...the kind of faith that founds not a religion of supplication, but a religion of good life conduct" (*Failure*, 8:267). It is no surprise that Kant should express himself in this way having done so twice in his early-Critical period. In *Lectures* we find "*moral theology* is something different from *theological morality*, namely, a morality in which the concept of obligation presupposes the concept of God" (*Lect*, 28:1002) whilst earlier, in the first *Critique*, there is:

> Not theological morals; for that contains moral laws that presuppose the existence of a highest governor of the world, whereas moral theology . . . is a conviction of the existence of a highest being which grounds itself on moral laws. (A632n)

What these views secure is vital to Kant's own theodicy. Whether described as faith or theology, Kant's religious stance is based on morality and, as fully demonstrated in the *Groundwork*, the moral law is based on our rationality.[6] For Kant, it is again *rational* faith in God which underpins his authentic theodicy, not a "God knows best" irrational fideism without intellectual foundation.

Before ending this consideration of authentic theodicy, there are two potential objections to Kant's use of Job's story which can be reasonably anticipated and which could signal possible inconsistencies in Kant's views. A pre-emptive response is possible in both cases. The first is Kant's use of the Book of Job from the Bible which would seem to disqualify Kant's example of an authentic theodicy as it based on a claimed revealed text, a source of moral heteronomy. This is a false trail. Not only has attention been drawn to his special use of "doctrinal," but Kant has also acknowledged the story to be only an allegory, a parable. The historical veracity of Job's story or the possibility of it being a divinely revealed text does not matter here. To achieve its purpose the story need be no more than that, a story by which Kant is illustrating what he considers to be the correct attitude to take in response to apparent moral inequity, namely placing one's trust in God's moral wisdom.

The second potential objection is weightier. When rejecting attempted theodicy Ia, Kant roundly condemned the idea that man and God play by different moral rules. However, toward the end of his consideration of Job's tale, Kant relates that God shows Job both "the beautiful side of creation" but also that "God thereby demonstrates an order and a maintenance of the whole which proclaim a wise creator, *even though his ways, inscrutable to us*, must at the same time remain hidden" (*Failure*, 8:266; emphasis added). *Prima facie*, a statement more inconsistent with Kant's rejection of theodicy Ia is difficult to imagine. Galbraith is also concerned by this passage and further leverages her concern to reinforce the view that there is only one moral law, a stance strongly supported in this study.

> All the more troubling then, that Kant, despite his aversion to traditional theodicies, should resort to such claims such as that God's ways "remain inscrutable for us." We would be mistaken, however, to interpret Kant's claim as an admission that human moral standards do not apply to the divine, or that God's justice is different from ours. (2006, 185)

If theodicy Ia was accepted it would imply that there is another moral law created by God (and unknown to us). This would be a form of voluntarism, diametrically opposed to Kant's position that autonomous reason is the moral law's only source. With Job, however, the context is changed; it is now one of practical reason, namely moral faith. If faith is belief plus trust, then Job's trust in God allows his incomprehension of God's ways without pretending to *know* them. Indeed, to my mind, if faith cannot be equated with knowledge as attested to by Kant, there must always be something which is not known or understood but which is the object of such trust. Indeed, Kant's hero Job is described as a man who "in the midst of the strongest doubts" (*Rel*, 8:267) was still able to affirm his moral faith; as Brachtendorf (2002, 83) puts it, Job had *Zweifelglauben*. Another potential resolution to this second objection is to differentiate between the moral law and God's moral wisdom in applying it. Kant's treatment of the Story of Job contains a disclaimer about our knowledge of the moral order with potentially profound implications. The relevant passage is that cited above from *Failure*, 8:266 which continues: "indeed already in the physical order of things and how much more in the connection of the latter with *the moral order (which is all the more impenetrable to our reason)*" (emphasis added). This remarkable claim seems to turn Kant's argumentation on its head, not only in *Failure* but in his Critical works, where moral order is defined by the moral law which for Kant is an expression of reason (cf. *GW*, 4:411). As previously emphasized, there are *not* two moralities, one for God and one for human beings. Seeskin stresses this too: "[f]or Kant there is no extraterrestrial morality known only to God. There is one moral law and it is as binding on God as it is on me" (1987, 237). However, if moral order is not the same as moral law, could the moral order be God's wisdom in applying the single moral law? I hold that, if it is, then the second objection can be dismissed in a way compatible with Kant's defense of Job. Kant argues that we cannot know God's moral wisdom in the sensible world since this would require that we have knowledge of its grounds in the intelligible world "and that is an insight to which no mortal can attain" (*Failure*, 8:264). Crucial to this was that "proof of the world-author's moral wisdom in the sensible world" could only be obtained by someone who "penetrates to the cognition of the supersensible [intelligible] world." From the *Groundwork* we know that the moral law is grounded in reason and there is only one moral law for God and humans alike. Therefore Kant's argument that God's artistic wisdom and His moral wisdom cannot be combined in this world only succeeds if God's moral wisdom is something other than the moral law. Otherwise, since we already know both the moral law and God's artistic wisdom in the sensible world through experience and observation, we would be already able to combine them without recourse to the intelligible world. From this, it can be inferred that God's moral wisdom is not a rival moral law but rather His application of that law. This, in essence, is what Job is doing; he is continuing to put his trust in God's moral wisdom thus described.

Having presented the Story of Job as an example of authentic theodicy, Kant ends his treatise with a section entitled "Concluding Remark" which abstracts important themes from what has gone before. It is not surprising that here Kant explores in detail the notion of sincerity since it is this quality that he finds most commendable in Job. It is also an essential component of authentic theodicy, Kant observing that it is a theodicy that "less depends on subtle reasoning than on sincerity in taking notice of the impotence of our reason" (*Failure*, 8:267). For Kant, sincerity is based on truthfulness which he holds is a subjective condition of believing what we say to be true. He contrasts this with truth which is the objective condition where "we compare what we say with the object of logical judgment (through the understanding)" (ibid.). From this Kant is able to define the lie as a declaration counter to truthfulness and not truth. This should come as no surprise when it is recalled that in the *Groundwork* Kant places morality firmly in the intention and not in an act's outcome. This leads Kant to consider the role of conscience and he rightly points out the incoherence of the notion of an erring conscience.

Without the datum provided by conscience our actions would be morally random and not even able to be described as (im)moral at all since accountability for our actions would be absent. The concepts of sincerity and conscience are then merged by Kant:

> I can indeed err in the judgment *in which I believe* to be right, for this belongs to the understanding which alone judges objectively (rightly or wrongly); but in the judgment *whether I in fact believe* to be right (or merely pretend it) I absolutely cannot be mistaken. (*Failure*, 8:268)

Kant applies this merger to religious belief and theodicy. His example is Job's friends where these said what they did not believe in an attempt to please God. Kant holds this to be lying with the lie "the most absurd (before a render of hearts [God]): it is also the most sinful" (*Failure*, 8:269). He also prefigures *Religion* in that he has little time for purely external religious observance and in condemning those who do not attend to the inward nature of their claimed beliefs.

> [I]f someone says to himself (or—what is one and the same in religious professions—before God) that *he believes*, without perhaps casting even a single glimpse into himself . . . then such a person *lies*. (*Failure*, 8:268)

This passage lends strong support to the claim that Kant is not a fideist. Failure to look inside himself and examine the basis of his faith in God's existence and the relationship with Him is the very last thing of which Kant could be accused whether in *Failure*, his earlier second *Critique*, or in *Religion* to follow. This passage above also has an echo of Socrates' "the unexamined life is not worth living"; for Kant, it is clear that the unexamined faith was not worth having.

By including his commentary on the Story of Job, Kant has offered us not only an example of the failure of theodicies based on speculative reason (the arguments of Job's friends) but also how only a non-philosophical theodicy based on trust in God could work. However, it could still be argued that Kant has, despite the foregoing, merely adopted the fideist position of blind trust in God's ways which he rejected so firmly, when considering theodicy Ia. I do not consider such an argument to be sound. We have already noted that the rejection of Ia was on the grounds of claimed knowledge of God but Kant is making his claim here based on practical, moral grounds and certainly not contradicting reason *tout court* as the fideist does. It is this move on Kant's part which creates the middle ground in the matter of reconciling God and evil. Kant is rejecting the simple disjunctive choice between theodicy based on theoretical/speculative reason and one with fideism as its basis. Indeed, he rejects both but advances the sought after reconciliation still based on reason. Byrne (2007, 123) offers a similar account of Kant's position in which he (Byrne) concedes that it is possible to allow a very thin line to be drawn between a theodicy based on moral faith and a faith based on a more fideistic hope that God will somehow make things alright.

DOES AUTHENTIC THEODICY SUCCEED?

An examination of Kant's authentic theodicy would not be complete, however, without testing it against his definition of theodicy (cf. *Failure*, 8:255). Three major concerns arise. First, whilst it is reason which sets out the charge against God, Kant's authentic theodicy seems not to respond in those terms. Rather it is based on putting one's trust in God's moral wisdom in the manner of Job. It can also be asked whether Kant in his authentic theodicy has fully addressed the one type of evil which I have argued remains in his taxonomy, namely, moral evil. Again, the example of authentic theodicy which Kant puts forward deals with the seeming injustice of Job's misfortunes but injustice is a mismatch in the relationship between moral behavior and happiness, whether between virtue and unhappiness or between transgression of the moral law and happiness. In his theodicy, Kant does not go to the root of the problem, rather stopping short and not offering a reasoned explanation for the co-existence of moral evil *per se* and a theistic God with the conventional moral attributes. Thus it could be argued, as Busche does, (cf. 2013, 236) that Kant has not met the challenge which he himself set.

Second, as Kant's authentic theodicy is the only one that he eventually advanced, it can also be asked whether this theodicy has left any other substantial charges against God unaddressed. I believe this to be the case. In *New Elucidation*, Kant's fictional character Caius raised the problem of God's foreknowledge. Whilst granting that men freely choose to commit moral evil, the problem is that an omniscient God nevertheless chose to create in the foreknowledge that moral evil would ensue from man's free choice and so He bears an indirect but ultimate responsibility for that evil. Now for that charge to stick it would require acceptance of the premise that to create under such circumstances is worse than not to create at all. God's defender could well claim the converse, namely that creation with the opportunity for evil is better than no creation at all. Further, any attempt to resolve this dilemma by asserting that God is an entity which *must* create would involve a knowledge claim about God inadmissible under Kant's critical epistemology. One possible solution is to disarm the problem and claim that foreknowledge applies to the future, a temporal concept. But the intelligible world of God is atemporal and thus foreknowledge is an incoherent anthropomorphic concept in that world.

The result would then be that previously identified by Neiman: "[i]n the process of defending God, [we have] disempowered Him" (2002, 26). Alternatively, God's foreknowledge could be denied *tout court* as in the Socinian heresy but this runs into the Neiman objection too. Regardless of the position taken with respect to this problem, the key issue for this study is that Kant's authentic theodicy does not even defend God on this charge let alone achieve the better result of demonstrating His innocence. Kant is silent on this issue.

Third, there is the lingering concern that, with his own authentic theodicy, Kant has still only introduced a variant on theodicy Ia which he rejected out of hand. It will be recalled that this theodicy was based on the notion of God having a different (but still unknown) system of moral law. In authentic theodicy, Kant appeals to God's moral wisdom (but still unknown) in applying the one moral law. Now, as already acknowledged, Kant's defender could say that in the first case the argument was based on inadmissible theoretical reason whilst in the second the argument was based on practical reason. That point can be granted without invalidating the claim they nevertheless can both be termed theodicies of ignorance. Drawing on the same property, Paul Rateau (2009, 65) characterizes authentic theodicy as one of postponement where the full understanding of God's moral wisdom is one of the rewards of the elect in the next life. Should Rateau's interpretation be correct, we can then note the similarity with theodicy IIIc which Kant rejected but which pointed to "a future world [where] a different order of things will obtain." Thus Kant could be accused of merely substituting another would-be theodicy of postponement for an earlier unsuccessful variant.

Nonetheless, Kant's Concluding Remark in *Failure* on sincerity needs to be fully weighed together with his earlier words: "the human being is justified, as rational, in testing all claims, all doctrines which impose respect on him, before he submits himself to them, so that this respect may be sincere and not feigned" (*Failure*, 8:255). In the light of these statements, the sincerity with which Kant is searching for a successful theodicy cannot, with good cause, be doubted. As we have seen, Kant, in his eyes, has been successful in discovering and describing a theodicy of the middle ground. However, this does not entail that the resultant authentic theodicy *per se* is a success.

The three concerns above relating to authentic theodicy are linked by a common thread. It has been emphasized at a number of places in this study that theodicy is concerned with finding a reasoned explanation which reconciles the apparently irreconcilable, namely God and evil. Much attention has been paid to showing that, for Kant, "reasoned" was well supported by the use of practical, moral, reason. But what remains of "explanation"? When we look again at the theodicies which Kant evaluated in Failure, a significant feature emerges. All nine philosophical theodicies were definitely offering an attempted explanation. Their failure was, at root, the failure of theoretical reason. However, with his own authentic theodicy, Kant is no longer offering any explanation. With the first concern listed above, Kant is offering no explanation for God's allowance of moral evil in the world. With the second, Kant is offering no explanation of why God chose to create knowing that evil would result. With the third, Kant is indeed offering no explanation, but rather offering just a means of coming to terms with the *lack* of an explanation of how moral evil and God could be compatible. His authentic theodicy is instead just based on trust in the moral wisdom of God. It is a means of getting-by in the face of moral evil which Rateau is correct in terming a theodicy of postponement. If there is a reconciliation occurring it seems to be one between man and evil, not God and evil. However, there are counters available to those who would reject the case put forward and would support Kant in this matter. The first is that that demanding an explanation merely takes us full circle back to philosophical theodicies. These try to provide an explanation but Kant has shown that they must fail and that they do so *necessarily*. It was exactly this failure which prompted his search for an alternative in the first place. The second possible counter is that Kant has dispensed with knowledge to make room for faith (cf. Bxxx) but a demand for an explanation is a demand for knowledge which Kant states *cannot* be supplied. However, these counters can be challenged in their turn, drawing on an unambiguous statement from Kant himself. Thirty-six years earlier in his pre-Critical period, Kant in *New Elucidation* confirmed the need for explanation:

> [T]he world contains a number of evils. What is being sought is not the ground *that,* in other words, not the grounds of knowing, for experience takes its place. What has to be specified is the ground *why*, that is to say, the ground of becoming. (*NE*, 1:392)

Thus setting aside these possible counters, I conclude that Kant has not met the challenge he set himself of constructing a successful theodicy. In reaching this conclusion it has not been necessary to challenge the moral faith upon which authentic theodicy is based. However, a significant challenge to Kant comes from such a direction. Although it cannot be dealt with comprehensively in this study, it would be a major omission to exclude the topic completely as it has the potential to provide additional grounds for the failure of authentic theodicy. A highly abridged version is offered.

Abundant evidence has been presented in this study that the faith which supports Kant's authentic theodicy is a moral faith. The object of that faith is a God whose existence has been postulated on moral grounds. Although Kant rehearses the argument in earlier works, it is in the second *Critique* where he makes his definitive move when he claims that we have a duty to variously pursue or achieve the Highest Good. Whilst the highest individual good for

Kant is the moral law, this Highest Good (*summum bonum*) is a synthesis of obedience to the moral law and happiness in proportion to that obedience. The introduction of a duty with respect to the Highest Good grounds Kant's two practical postulates. If we have a duty, we have an "ought" and for Kant we cannot have a duty which is impossible to discharge. He then considers the conditions which are required for this. First, he recognises that this duty cannot be discharged in the present world; a future one is needed and thus he postulates immortality. Second, he acknowledges that one individual cannot judge the degree of compliance with the moral law by another. An entity is needed who can see unerringly into an individual's heart. This entity is God. Thus Kant has established to his satisfaction that God can be postulated on moral grounds and thus the correct attitude toward Him is one of moral faith.

However, the Highest Good is perhaps the most controversial aspect of Kant's moral philosophy. The debate about it is extensive with a long pedigree and is still an active issue at the time of writing.[7] There are several aspects of the Highest Good which risk undermining the moral faith on which Kant's authentic theodicy is built. Some of these are now set out in summary. There is disagreement whether the Highest Good is to be achieved in this world or a future one. Some scholars agree that the Highest Good is a useful concept but one to be realised in this world.[8] Whilst such a secular Highest Good is a worthwhile social goal, I contend that it is not the one envisaged by Kant. If the Highest Good could be achieved in this world, immortality and God would not require postulation. This could not have been Kant's intention as this would defeat his continuing aim of securing a place for God in his philosophical system.

Some scholars hold that a duty with respect to the Highest Good has not been established or that it has not been established with the same rigour with which the duty to obey the moral law was established, namely *a priori*.[9] Criticism of the duty also includes the charge that it is redundant as it introduces no new obligation above that to obey the moral law; the various formulations of the Categorical Imperative suffice.[10] Other criticisms are that the duty is introduced for purely theological purposes[11] and that happiness has been falsely re-introduced as a motive for obeying the moral law, it having been dismissed as such by Kant in the *Groundwork*.

Should it be granted that there is indeed a duty in respect to the Highest Good, the manner of its fulfilment produces further dispute. One aspect of this focuses on the nature of the future world. Kant is insistent that we behave morally only when we have the opportunity to do otherwise and give in to inadmissible sensible inclinations. However, the future world is purely intelligible and thus free of those inclinations which could lead to transgress the moral law. Therefore we cannot be moral in the sense meant by Kant and so are incapable of the moral development which would eventually be rewarded by happiness in proper proportion.

In sum, these concerns are enough for some scholars to hold that Kant's moral faith is not soundly based. If that is the case, then the foundation for authentic theodicy would fall away. This issue is held open in this study as I hold that it is not necessary to appeal to the failure of the Highest Good to show that authentic theodicy does not succeed. The grounds for this are those set out above.

NOTES

1. Although Duncan (2012) and I have differed on the route by which Kant reached this point and the timing of Kant's conclusion, we agree on his stance on evil in 1791.

2. In addition to giving us the clearest indication that Kant will base any eventual theodicy on morality it also reprises Kant's dismissal of the traditional proofs of God's existence based as they all are in Kant's view on the ontological argument.

3. A change of basis is also detected by Cassirer (1932, 151) in his review of the philosophy of the enlightenment and who holds that the basis for theodicy was no longer to be found in metaphysics.

4. Matter or concern of faith.

5. Loades' (1985, 42) holds that Kant also had a political aim in his consideration of Job. *Failure* was written after the accession of Frederick William II of Prussia and the appointment of Wöllner as Minister of Culture which led to the reduction of religious freedom through censorship edicts and the setting up of courts of theological examination. Loades considers that Wöllner and his circle were the target of one of Kant's conclusions: "before any court of dogmatic theologians, before a synod, an inquisition, a venerable congregation, or any higher consistory in our times (one alone excepted), Job would have suffered a sad fate" (*Failure*, 8:266).

6. Well expressed by Byrne (2007, 95) as "[r]espect for the impartial, universal demands of reason of itself gives moral law authority."

7. For example, see Bader (2015) and Pasternak (2017).

8. For example, see Reath (1988).

9. For example, see Lewis White Beck (1960).

10. For example, see Stephen Engstrom (1992, 776ff., 779).

11. For example, see Auxter (1979, 121ff.).

Conclusion

In the Introduction I tabled the major theses for which I would be arguing. Having completed the examination of Kant's thought on theodicy, the key conclusions for each of the six theses are now brought together here.

(a). Kant had a career-long concern with theodicy.

This was the thesis that motivated and underpinned the whole study. This concern with theodicy was a manifestation of Kant's effort, also career-long, to secure a place for God in his philosophical system but one still subject to the primacy of reason. Kant's career has been examined in three distinct periods, the pre-Critical, early-Critical, and late-Critical. In each, it was seen there was much of theodical relevance. In the first period, his concern started in Reflections 3703–5 from 1753/1754 and was set in the context of Leibniz's theodicy. In 1759 he endorsed one key element of that theodicy, the best possible world. Thereafter, his thinking reflected on the three major elements required for a theodicy, the existence of God, the nature of evil, and the freedom of human action together with the interaction between these elements. In the second period, his thought evolved, retaining some elements from the pre-Critical period, changing others, and introducing new elements that would come to full bloom in the third period. However, at the end of the second period there were significant unresolved tensions in matters relevant to any theodicy he might advance. These primarily lay in the seeming inconsistencies between the first *Critique* and views recorded in the later *Lectures*. His epistemology had run ahead of his thought on theodicy. In the final period, epistemology and theodicy were brought into alignment when Kant adopted his definitive stance on theodicy in the 1791 treatise *Failure*. There, consistent with the Critical epistemology, he rejected all philosophical theodicies but advanced his own "authentic" version based on practical reason. This was immediately followed by his last work of major theodical relevance, *Religion*. In this, he set down his ultimate view on evil, one of theodicy's essential elements. On the basis of the evidence presented in the study and summarized here, I hold that Kant did indeed have a career-long concern with theodicy. This concern manifested itself in the following ways.

(b). Kant's stance on theodicy developed throughout his career.

Kant was concerned with the nature of both God and evil and the relationship between the two throughout his career even though he did not formally draw them together or use the word "theodicy" until *Failure*. Kant's thought on theodicy was continuous in the sense of career-long but discontinuous in the sense of the far-reaching change wrought with *Failure*. The relationship between God and evil was not static for Kant. His efforts to establish a definitive stance on this relationship under the condition of freedom form an extended search for the reasoned explanation that must ground an effective theodicy. The context in which theodicy was situated at the start of his career was provided by Leibniz's *Theodicy* but he slowly distanced himself from this. It was established that in both his pre-Critical and early-Critical periods Kant held that philosophical theodicies were possible but what such a theodicy consisted in was subject to development. He definitively broke with Leibniz's theodicy and philosophical theodicies in general in *Failure*.

(c). Kant did not reject all theodicies.

This can be regarded as a corollary of (b). Kant certainly rejected philosophical theodicies where "philosophical" is taken in special sense of "theoretical, speculative" but advanced his own authentic theodicy. However, an argument that he did not reject all theodicies can only succeed once Kant's expansion of the area covered by "theodicy" is allowed. It was no longer just the attempted reconciliation through theoretical, speculative, reason of the apparent incompatibility between the presence of evil and God. It now also encompassed the effort to provide a reasoned explanation underpinned by practical, moral, reason. In advancing his authentic theodicy, Kant found a middle ground between the philosophical theodicies which he rejected and the fideism which was equally unacceptable to him.

(d). Kant's work in other areas constrained his theodicy.

Several constraints were identified which had the cumulative effect of circumscribing Kant's eventual explicit theodicy, "authentic" theodicy, and limiting it to the moral sphere. There were two principal constraints, the first of which emerged in the pre-Critical period. With his adoption of Newtonian principles in *Universal Natural History*, Kant came to see that what had been regarded as physical evil was not so. Nature was morally indifferent. That the operation of the universal and unchanging laws of nature brought suffering to humans was not in doubt, but it was not evil. As such, it could not be divine punishment for moral evil. For this reason, such natural harm no longer had to be accounted for in a theodicy. The second major constraint came from the Critical epistemology in which Kant established the boundary to our knowledge, showing that knowledge of God is beyond our reach. Whilst this epistemology clearly impacted much more than just theodicy in Kant's subsequent thought, the specific effect on would-be theodicies was that those reliant on claimed knowledge of God must fail of necessity.

(e). Metaphysical Evil conceived as limitation and Radical Evil perform the same function.

Kant's stance on evil evolved through his career. In *Negative Magnitudes*, whilst still retaining metaphysical evil conceived as limitation in the Leibnizian tradition, Kant now saw a class of evil that was ontologically real but with a negative value when compared to the good. In *Lectures*, Kant appeared to revert to his original stance. However, when the notion of radical evil, as advanced in *Religion*, was examined, it was found to perform the same function as Leibnizian metaphysical evil conceived as limitation, namely that of being the ground of the possibility of evil. Neither was evil itself. In this way, Kant's rejection in *Failure* of metaphysical evil as morally accountable was given added weight. Further, for Kant, by elimination, the real evil to be reconciled with God's properties in any theodicy was now confined to just one type, that done by humans, moral evil. By doing that Kant, significantly and correctly, directed our search for the source of evil inwards to ourselves rather than outwards into the metaphysics of Creation or the workings of nature. I consider that if this was the only result of Kant's consideration of theodicy throughout his career it alone would be enough to make such an exercise on his part of inestimable value regardless of the success (or otherwise) of his "authentic" theodicy.

(f). Kant's authentic theodicy fails.

This forms the culminating thesis to this study. As Kant held that previous, philosophical, theodicies had failed, it was essential that his own theodicy should also be fully investigated to establish whether it succeeded and, if yes, to what extent. Authentic theodicy does not meet the requirement of Kant's own definition that a reasoned explanation is given which reconciled the apparently irreconcilable, namely the counter-purposive and a theistic God. Whilst it was reasoned in that it depended on practical (as opposed to theoretical) reason, it only addressed injustice which concerns the *relationship* between moral evil and (un)happiness.

Authentic theodicy does not tackle the underlying issue of moral evil, the allowance of which by God is left unaddressed. Instead, authentic theodicy just urges trust in God's moral wisdom in applying the one moral law, a would-be theodicy of postponement. In addition, it did not tackle the issue, ever-present from Kant's pre-Critical days, of why an omniscient God would choose to create a world knowing that evil would result. That man was directly responsible for moral evil does not address God's indirect but ultimate responsibility.

CONSEQUENCES OF FAILURE

However, this summary cannot suffice as the conclusion to this study. It must be asked what hinges on these findings—the ever-present "so what?" question. Two issues must be addressed before the study can properly be drawn to a close. First, the wider significance and consequences of authentic theodicy's failure must be marked out in general terms. Second, whether anything can be salvaged from its failure must be determined. Whilst these two issues cannot be fully addressed within the scope available to this study, neither can they be altogether ignored.

In particular, it must be asked if moral faith *per se* can survive the failure of authentic theodicy. The answer depends on whether moral faith can be separated from rational faith. In one sense, by endeavoring to show that his faith was rational, Kant wanted to have his cake and eat it. A suitable illustration of the latter can be seen in a citation highlighted previously, that "no one will ever be able to boast that he *knows* there is a God and a future life. No, the conviction is not *logical* but *moral* certainty" (A828/B856; emphasis in original). Kant is here still appealing to a form a certainty but one that nevertheless falls short of knowledge. As Brachtendorf puts it, Kant's *Glaubenssache* possesses a lower level of certainty when compared with knowledge (cf. 2002, 64). Furthermore, moral faith is being equated by Kant with moral certainty, but faith with complete certainty would no longer be faith. Kant had no choice but to follow his own epistemology and deny knowledge of God. However, he wanted at the same time to hang on to something certain in place of knowledge, something which was less than it in the theoretical sense but equated with it in another, practical sense. We recall that the fundamental tenet of authentic theodicy is the placing one's trust in God's moral wisdom. There is nothing to stop a person still doing that but on the basis of a different kind of faith to the one envisaged by Kant. After all, when Job put his trust in God's moral wisdom, notwithstanding all indications to the contrary, he did not do so supported by Kant's construction of moral faith; he just put his trust in God's moral judgment pure and simple. Job's is still a moral faith but it is not one which meets the characteristics of moral faith as set out by Kant. A related question is the following: now that authentic theodicy as constructed by Kant has been seen to fail, does that mean the end of theodicy taken in the widened sense employed by Kant? I judge not. Rather what has happened is that Kant's famous statement at Bxxx now has a strengthened meaning. The failure of authentic theodicy means that, in addition to Kant denying knowledge, *all* forms of certainty in matters of faith must be dispensed with. Theodicy can still survive. Let it be called fundamental theodicy; it is the theodicy of Job, a theodicy of trust and patience but this is no longer the reasoned explanation which Kant sought. Indeed theodicy is truly now a *Glaubenssache*. As is fitting, I leave the final word of this study to Kant. The failure of authentic theodicy and possibly that of the moral proof does not mean that his statement below has lost any of its power:

> This commanded action [the Highest Good] taken *together with the only conditions of its possibility conceivable for us*, namely God's existence and the soul's immortality, are *matters of faith* (*res fidei*) and moreover are the only ones which can be so termed amongst all objects (*CPJ*, 5:469; author's translation; emphasis in original)

Bibliography

Alexander, H. (ed.). (1956). *The Leibniz-Clarke correspondence.* Manchester: Manchester University Press.
Allison, H. E. (July 1986). Morality and Freedom: Kant's Reciprocity Thesis. *The Philosophical Review, XCV, No. 3*, 393–425.
Allison H. E. (1990). *Kant's Theory of Freedom.* Cambridge: Cambridge University Press
Ameriks, K. (2012). *Kant's Elliptical Path.* Oxford: Oxford University Press.
Antognazza, M.-R. (2009). *Leibniz An Intellectual Biography.* New York: Cambridge University Press.
Antognazza, M.-R. (2014). Metaphysical Evil Revisited. In L. M. Jorgensen and S. Newlands, *New Essays on Leibniz's Theodicy* (pp. 112–135). Oxford: Oxford University Press.
Auxter, T. (1979). The Unimportance of Kant's Highest Good. *Journal of the History of Philosophy*, 121–134.
Bader, R. M. (2015). Kant's Theory of the Highest Good. In J. Aufderheide and R. M. Bader (eds.), *The Highest Good in Aristotle and Kant* (pp. 183–213). Oxford, Oxford University Press.
Beck, L. W. (1960). *A Commentary on Kant's Critique of Practical Reason.* Chicago: University of Chicago Press.
Beck, L. W. (1969). *Early German Philosophy—Kant and His Predecessors.* Cambridge, MA: Harvard University Press.
Beiser, F. C. (1987). *The Fate of Reason—German Philosophy from Kant to Fichte.* Cambridge, MA: Harvard University Press.
Beiser, F. C. (2006). Moral Faith and the Highest Good. In P. Guyer (ed.), *The Cambridge Companion to Kant and Modern Philosophy* (pp. 588–629). Cambridge: Cambridge University Press.
Blackburn, S. (2008). *Oxford Dictionary of Philosophy* (2nd ed. revised). Oxford: Oxford University Press.
Brachtendorf, J. (2002). Kants Theodizee-Aufsatz-Die Bedingungen des Gelingens philosophischer Theodizee. *Kant-Studien*, 57–83.

Busche, H. (2013). Kant's Kritik der Theodizee - Eine Metakritik. In W. L.-B. (Eds), *Studia Leibnitiana - Supplementa Band 36* (pp. 231–269). Franz Steiner Verlag.
Byrne, P. (2007). *Kant on God*. Aldershot: Ashgate.
Cassirer, E. (1918). *Kants Leben und Lehre* (Translated by James Haden 1981 *Kant's Life and Thought*). New Haven: Yale University Press.
Cassirer, E. (1951). *The Philosophy of the Enlightenment*. Princeton, NJ: Princeton University Press.
Caswell, M. (2006). Kant's Conception of the Highest Good, the Gesinnung, and the Theory of Radical Evil. *Kant-Studien*, 184–209.
Cavallar, G. (1993). Kants Weg von der Theodizee zur Anthropodizee und retour. *Kant-Studien*, 90–102.
Caygill, H. (1995). *A Kant Dictionary*. Malden MA: Blackwell.
Chignell, A. (2007). Belief in Kant. *Philosophical Review*, 323–360.
Despland, M. (1973). *Kant on History and Religion*. Montreal: McGill—Queen's University Press.
DiCenso, J. (2012). *Kant's Religion within the Boundaries of Mere Reason—A Commentary*. New York: Cambridge University Press.
Duncan, S. (2012). Moral Evil, Freedom and the Goodness of God: Why Kant Abandoned Theodicy. *British Journal for the History of Philosophy 20(5)*, 973–991.
Engel, E. J. (2004). Mendelssohn contra Kant. *Kant Studien*, 269–282.
Engstrom, S. (1992). The Concept of the Highest Good in Kant's Moral Theory. *Philosophy and Phenomenological Research 52(4)*, 747–780.
Etcheverria, M. T. (1976). La Teodica del Kant Precritio. *Pensamiento*, 157–180.
Fackenheim, E. (1996). *The God Within, Kant, Schelling, and Historicity*. Toronto: University of Toronto Press.
Fonnesu, L. (2006). The Problem of Theodicy. In K. Haaksonssen, *The Cambridge History of Eighteen Century Philosophy* (pp. 749–778). Cambridge: Cambridge University Press.
Galbraith, E. (2006). Kant and "A Theodicy of Protest." In C. L. Firestone and S. R. Palmquist (eds.), *Kant and the New Philosophy of Religion* (pp. 179–189). Bloomington: Indiana University Press.
Heimsoeth, H. (1966). Zum Kosmotheologischen Ursprung der Kantischen Freiheitsantinomie. *Kant Studien, Vol 57.1*, 206–229.
Hick, J. (2007). *Evil and the God of Love*. Basingstoke: Palgrave Macmillan.
Insole, C. (2008). The Irreducible Importance of Religious Hope in Kant's Conception of the Highest Good. *Philosophy*, 333–351.
Kant, Immanuel.Works are cited by volume and page number of Kant's *Gesammelte Schriften* (AA, edited by the German Academy of Sciences, Berlin, 1900–), the *Akademie Ausgabe*. Except for the translations of the earthquake essays and Living Forces, all the translations to English are from the *Cambridge Edition of the Works of Immanuel Kant*, General Editors Paul Guyer and Allen Wood, Cambridge: Cambridge University Press (1992 onward)

The works cited and the abbreviations used in attribution are:

LF: Thoughts on the true estimation of Living Forces . . .
Refl: *Reflexionen zur Metaphysik 3703–3705*—Three manuscript reflections on optimism.

NE:	A New Elucidation of the First Principles of Metaphysical Cognition.
OPA:	The Only Possible Argument in Support of a Demonstration of the Existence of God.
UNH:	Universal Natural History and Theory of the Heavens, or Essay on the Constitution and Mechanical Origin of the Entire Universe, treated in accordance with Newtonian Principles.
EE2:	History and natural description of the most noteworthy occurences of the earthquake that struck a large part of the Earth at the end of the year 1755.
Opt:	Attempt at Some Reflections on Optimism.
NM:	Attempt to Introduce the Concept of Negative Magnitudes in Philosophy.
DP:	Inquiry concerning the distinctness of the principles of natural theology and morality.
Lect:	Lectures on Philosophical Theology.
Idea:	Idea for a Universal Natural History with a Cosmopolitan Aim.
GW:	Groundwork of the Metaphysics of Morals.
CB:	Conjectural Beginning of Human History.
CPR:	Critique of Practical Reason.
CPJ:	Critique of the Power of Judgement.
Failure:	On the Miscarriage of All Philosophical Trials.
Rel:	Religion within the Boundaries of Mere Reason and Other Writings.
SF:	The Conflict of the Faculties.
MM:	The Metaphysics of Morals.
LM:	Lectures on Metaphyics.

Exception is made for *Critique of Pure Reason*, where the convention Annn/Bnnn is followed, indicating the page number of the first and second editions respectively.

Kanzian, C. (1993). Kant und Crusius 1763. *Kant Studien*, 399–407.

Korsgaard, C. M. (1996). *Creating the Kingdom of Ends*. Cambridge: Cambridge University Press.

Kremer, J. (1909). Das Problem der Theodizee in der Philosophie und Literatur des 18. Jahrhunderts mit besonderer Rücksicht auf Kant und Schiller. In *Kantstudien-Ergänzungshefte* (p. Bd.13). Berlin: W. de Gruyter.

Kuehn, M. (2001). *Kant: A Biography*. Cambridge: Cambridge University Press.

Larrimore, M. (2004). Autonomy and the Invention of Theodicy. In N. B. (eds.), *New Essays on the History of Autonomy* (pp. 61–92). Cambridge: Cambridge University Press.

Leibniz, G. (1710). *Theodicy*. Translated by E.M. Huggard. La Salle, IL: Open Court (1985).

Loades, A. (1985). *Kant and Job's Comforters*. Newcastle upon Tyne: Avero Publications.

Loades, A. (1975). Kant's Concern with Theodicy. *The Journal of Theological Studies*, 361–376.

Murray, Michael and Greenberg, Sean, "Leibniz on the Problem of Evil," *The Stanford Encyclopedia of Philosophy* (Spring 2013 Edition), Edward N. Zalta (ed.),

URL = <http://plato.stanford.edu/archives/spr2013/entries/leibniz-evil/>. Accessed November 23, 2014.

Nadler, S. (2008). Theodicy and Providence. In S. Nadler and T. M. Rudavsky (eds.), *Cambridge History of Jewish Philosophy, Vol.1* (pp. 619–658). Cambridge: Cambridge University Press.

Neiman, S. (2002). *Evil in Modern Thought*. Princeton NJ: Princeton University Press.

Palmquist, S. R. (2000). *Kant's Critical Religion*, Vol. 2. Aldershot: Ashgate.

Pasternack, L. (2011). The Development and Scope of Kantian Belief: The Highest Good, The Practical Postulates and the Fact of Reason. *Kant-Studien*, 290–315.

Pasternack, L. (2017). Restoring Kant's Conception of the Highest Good, *Journal of the History of Philosophy 55(3)*, 435–468.

Pope, A. (1994). *Essay on Man & Other Poems*. Mineola, NY: Dover Publications Inc.

Rateau, P. (2009). L'essai leibnizien de theodicee et la critique de Kant. In P. R. (ed.), *L'idee de theodicee de Leibniz a Kant: heritage, transformations, critiques* (pp. 51–66). Stuttgart: Franz Steiner Verlag.

Reardon, B. M. (1988). *Kant as Philosophical Theologian*. Basingstoke: Macmillan.

Reath, A. (1988). Two Conceptions of the Highest Good in Kant. *Journal of the History of Philosophy*, 593–619.

Schnepf, R. (2001). Metaphysik oder Metaphysikkritik? Das Kausalitätsproblem in Kants Abhandlung Über die negativen Größen. *Archiv fur Geschichte der Philosophie*, 130–159.

Schönfeld, M. (2000). *The Philosophy of the Young Kant*. New York: Oxford University Press.

Schulte, C. (1991). Zweckwidriges in der Erfahrung, Zur Genese des Misslingens aller philosophischen Versuche in der Theodizee bei Kant. *Kant-Studien*, 371–396.

Seeskin, K. (1987). Job and the Problem of Evil. *Philosophy and Literature*, 226–241.

Silber, J. R. (1959). Kant's Conception of the Highest Good as Immanent and Transcendent. *The Philosophical Review*, 469–492.

Silber, J. R. (1974). Procedural Formalism in Kant's Ethics. *The Review of Metaphysics*, 197–236.

Theis, R. (2009). La question de l'optimisme dans la premiere pensee de Kant. In P. R. (ed.), *L'idee de theodicee de Leibniz a Kant: heritage, transformations, critiques* (pp. 157–164). Stuttgart: Franz Steiner Verlag.

Vaihinger, H. (1911). *The Philosophy of "As if."* London: Harcourt Brace & Co.

Vailati, E. (1997). *Leibniz & Clarke*. New York: Oxford University Press.

Voltaire. (1759). *Candide*. London: Penguin Popular Classics (2001).

Wood, A. W. (1970). *Kant's Moral Religion*. Ithaca: Cornell University Press.

Yakira, E. (2009). Du mal metaphysique au mal radical: Leibniz, Kant, et la fin des theodicees. In P. Rateau, *L'idee de theodicee de Leibniz a Kant: heritage, transformations, critiques* (pp. 147–156). Stuttgart: Franz Steiner Verlag.

Zinkin, M. (2012). Kant on Negative Magnitudes. *Kant Studien*, 397–414.

Index

absentia, 28–29, 32
absurdum practicum, 75
Alexander the Great, 102
antecedent will, 4, 44, 66, 82, 98, 100
Antognazza, M-R., 14, 114
artistic wisdom, 107–8, 128
authentic theodicy, xii, xvi–xvii, xix–xx, 5, 41, 74, 77, 86, 91, 109, 112, 121–34, 136–39

Baumgarten, A., 49–53, 87
Beraubung, 27
best possible world, ix, 3–4, 9–11, 23, 44–45, 62–64, 80–81, 88, 94, 135
Böse, 24, 95, 97, 100, 107–8
Brachtendorf, J., 81, 98, 114, 124, 127, 138
Busche, H., 14, 97–98, 100–101, 106, 113, 118, 130
Byrne, P., 109, 130

Candide (Voltaire), ix, 5
Canon of Pure Reason, The, 54, 74
Cassirer, E., 11, 101
Chignell, A., 25
compossibility, 7–8, 45
Conjectural Beginning (Kant), 47–50, 52–53, 65, 67, 69, 79

consequent will, 4, 44, 82, 98, 100
Copernican turn, xix, 37, 47, 54, 73, 79–80
cosmological proof, 9, 39, 41, 57.
  See also proof of God's existence
counter-purposive, x, xii, 30, 93–98, 101, 103, 113, 119
Crusius, 11, 25–26, 34, 38, 62

defense of God, 7, 34, 44, 80, 95.
  See also free-will defense
deism, 19
determining ground, 34, 43
DiCenso, J., 115
doctrinal theodicy, xvii, 123, 127
Doctrine of the Elements, 50, 84

earthquake essays (Kant), 5, 20, 22–23, 31, 45, 75
Essay on Man (Pope), 3, 16, 37
evil as limitation, xvii–xix, 24, 29–31, 45, 83, 99, 107, 111–12, 114, 117–18, 137

Failure (Kant), ix–x, xi–xii, xvi–xvii, xix, 6, 12, 21–22, 24, 30, 32, 54, 62, 69, 72–75, 79, 81–82, 91–109, 111–13, 118–19, 122–37
fideism, ix, xvi, 124–26, 129, 136

first *Critique* (Kant), 9, 37–38, 40, 46, 50–56, 59, 61–62, 70, 72–74, 76, 80, 84–85, 87–89, 95, 98, 104–5, 107–8, 121–24, 126, 135
Frederick the Great, 88
Frederick William II, xii, 134
free-will defense, 44–45, 69
freedom, xviii, 1, 16, 30, 32–37, 43–44, 46, 55, 62, 69, 82, 100, 104–5, 108, 113–16, 118–19, 122, 134–36
free-will theodicy, 66, 82

Genghis Khan, 101
Gesinnung, 115
Glaubenssache, 124, 138–39
God as a regulative ideal, 85–86
God's artistic wisdom, 107–8, 128
God's foreknowledge, 36, 38, 45, 66, 130–31
God's justice, ix, x, 11, 21, 24, 30 75, 96, 98, 125–27
Gordian Knot, 102
greater good theodicy, 44–45, 66, 102
ground of evil, xvii, 117–18

highest good, xv, 5, 49, 54, 64, 73, 74–77, 81, 89, 104–5, 108–9, 125, 132–34, 139

Idea (Kant), 47–50, 52–55, 65, 68–69, 76, 79, 81
ideal of pure reason, 55, 84, 86, 88, 95, 108
instrumental theodicy, 44, 53, 66, 68, 81

Job, story of, xv, 21–22, 125–30, 138–39

Kuehn, M., 11, 40

laws of nature, xviii, 1, 7, 14–15, 17–24, 45, 59–61, 64–65, 96, 102, 104
lazy reason, 61, 63, 65, 82
Lectures (Kant), 47, 49–53, 57, 59–62, 65–67, 69–73, 75–77, 79–81, 86–89,
96, 99, 103, 109, 111–12, 117–18, 126, 135, 137
Leibniz, G. W., ix–x, xvi–xvii, 1, 3–15, 18, 20–24, 31–32, 37, 39, 44–45, 63–64, 66, 70, 82, 96, 98, 100–101, 109, 112–14, 118, 135–36
limited view theodicy, 6, 80
Lisbon earthquake, 15, 20, 23
Living Forces (Kant), 15
Loades, A., 9, 19, 40

mala defectus, 28
mala privationis, 28
Mangel, 28
Maupertuis, 3, 101
metaphysical evil, xvii, 4, 13–14, 29, 83, 99, 111–14, 117–19, 122 137
miracles, 15, 19, 22–24, 42, 45–46, 60
moral development process, 66
moral evil, x, xvii–xviii, 4–7, 13–15, 21–24, 30–31, 33–34, 37, 44, 60, 65, 67, 80, 82, 84–85, 91, 95–100, 102–3, 105, 108, 111–14, 117–18, 121–22, 130, 132, 137–38
moral faith, xvi, xx, 54, 74, 104, 122, 127, 130, 132–34, 138–39
moral law, xi, 22, 46, 48, 67, 70–78, 82, 85–86, 88, 93, 96–98, 104, 115–17, 121, 124, 126–28, 130–31, 133–34, 138
moral progression theodicy, 81
moral proof, 38, 72, 122, 139
moral wisdom, 106–8, 127–32, 138

natural harm, 23, 45, 60, 95, 102–3, 118, 121, 137
necessitation, xviii, 1, 4–5, 7–8, 18, 24, 34, 36, 41, 51, 62, 71, 86, 99, 137
Negative Magnitudes (Kant) 8, 12, 25–26, 29–32, 45, 83, 100, 111–12, 117–18
Neiman, S., 7, 131
net good theodicy, 5
New Elucidation (Kant), 38–39, 42–43, 62, 99, 130, 132

Newton, Sir I., xviii, 19, 23
noumenal moral agency, 115

Only Possible Argument (Kant), 8, 12, 15, 20, 22–23, 37, 39–43, 45, 57, 87
ontological argument, 9, 40, 56–57
ontology of evil, 118
optimism, xiv, xviii, 3, 5, 7–9, 11, 15, 20, 37 39
Optimism (Kant), 3–4, 7, 9–12, 18, 30, 42, 45, 62

philosophical theodicy, xi, xix, 22, 79–80, 82. *See also* doctrinal theodicy
physical evil, x, 4–6, 13–14, 21, 23–24, 30–31, 37, 60, 95, 100, 103, 113–14, 118, 121, 137
physico-theological proof, 9, 57, 73. *See also* proof of God's existence
Pope, A., xi, 3, 6–7, 9, 15–16, 21–23, 37, 44
practical reason, xvi–xvii, 73, 96–97, 104–5, 107–9, 124–25, 127, 131, 133, 136–37
predisposition to the good, 65, 116–17
problem of evil, ix, 10, 100
proof of God's existence, 4, 6, 9, 38–42, 73
propensity to evil, 29, 113, 115–18
Prussian Royal Academy, 3, 6

radical evil, xvii, 91, 112–18, 137
Rateau, P., 131–32

Reflections (Kant), 3–4, 6, 10–12, 15–16, 21, 42, 44, 135
Religion (Kant), 29–30, 57–58, 65, 71, 76, 91, 112–13, 115–18, 129, 136–37

Schönfeld, M., 11–12, 16, 20, 30, 52
second *Critique*, 24, 38, 54, 56, 72, 74–76, 96, 104, 108–9, 129, 132
sincerity, xii, xx, 51, 122, 128–29, 131
Socrates, 129

taxonomy of evil, xvii, xix, 4, 12–14, 24–25, 30–31, 33, 85, 95, 97, 100, 109, 111–12, 118, 130
teleological proof, 41. *See also* proof of God's existence
telic centerpiece, 17
theoretical reason, xi, xvii, 56–57, 61, 72, 74, 91, 96, 104–5, 108, 131, 137
third *Critique*, 72

Übel, 24, 95, 97, 100, 107–8
Universal Natural History (Kant), 5, 15–18, 20–23, 31, 37, 41, 60–61, 136
unsocial sociability, 68

Vaihinger, H., 70–71
Voltaire, ix, 5

worthiness to be happy, 64, 75

Zinkin, M., 25

About the Author

After an information technology career, working for a US multinational, **George Huxford** returned to study at King's College, London, where he was awarded a PhD. His particular interests are the philosophy of religion and Kant's moral philosophy. His most recent publication is "Kant's Journey on Evil" in *Evil: A History*, edited by A. Chignell (2018).

www.ingramcontent.com/pod-product-compliance
Lightning Source LLC
Chambersburg PA
CBHW050908300426
44111CB00010B/1435